Why Texas

Why
Texas

How Business Discovered the Lone Star State

Ed Curtis Jr.

BROWN BOOKS
PUBLISHING GROUP

Why Texas
How Business Discovered the Lone Star State

Brown Books Publishing Group
16250 Knoll Trail Drive, Suite 205
Dallas, Texas 75248
www.BrownBooks.com
(972) 381-0009

A New Era in Publishing®

Publisher's Cataloging-In-Publication Data

Names: Curtis, Ed (Ed Gaines), 1967- author.
Title: Why Texas : how business discovered the Lone Star state / Ed Curtis Jr.
Description: Dallas, Texas : Brown Books Publishing Group, [2019]
Identifiers: ISBN 9781612543314
Subjects: LCSH: Business relocation--Texas--21st century. | Business
    enterprises--Texas--21st century. | Texas--Economic conditions$--21st
    century.
Classification: LCC HD58 .C87 2019 | DDC 338.6/04209764--dc23

ISBN 978-1-61254-331-4
LCCN 2019939659

Printed in the United States
10 9 8 7 6 5 4 3 2 1

For more information or to contact the author, please go to
www.EdCurtisJr.com.

I dedicate this book to Margaret Greene Cardone, my late aunt, who inspired me to move to Texas—and who, at the young age of forty-six, passed away nine months after my move. Aunt Margaret, I hope you like this book.

Contents

PART THREE: Takeaways

Chapter 21
Your Cheat Sheet

Chapter 22
Some Fun-Loving Texas "Ediquette"

About the Author

Acknowledgments

My thanks to Brown Books for sharing my passion about Texas and to Tom Reale, company president, for encouraging me to write this book sooner rather than later. To my editor, Bonnie Hearn Hill, thanks for your teamwork, mentorship, and enthusiasm. If you decide to relocate, I'll meet you at the runway.

I would like to thank my loved ones, who have supported me through the years from home and afar. My soul mate and wife, Staci, who supported and encouraged me to write this book. You are my inspiration and the love of my life. My children, Olivia and Eddie, who are the lights of my life and my pride and joy. My mother, Joan, who has always believed in me and instilled in me the confidence to follow my dreams. Her unconditional love and support has enabled me to be the man I am. My father, Ed Sr., whose name I am honored to carry, has been my lifelong role model. My younger brother and sisters, John, Jennifer, and Janine, whom I admire for their successes and miss every single day. Aunt Marie and my entire family at the Compound in Greenville, where my happiest childhood days resided. My family in Atlanta and Albany, Georgia; thank you for your love and support. I would also like to thank those in my extended family whom I never got to know as much as I'd have liked because of my move. I hope to change that after this book. Lastly, my cousin Chris Cardone and his late brother Billy, who I know miss Margaret more than I do.

Special thanks to Todd Short, my chief officer, friend, and confidant, who is like a brother and has always had my back. You've been there for me during the good times and bad. I will never forget that.

Thank you to all of the YTexas partners and friends. Without you, I could not have pulled off this book.

Milli Brown: CEO, Brown Books Publishing Group

G. Brint Ryan: Chairman and CEO, Ryan LLC

Donnie Nelson: General Manager, Dallas Mavericks

Ralph Hawkins: Chairman Emeritus, HKS

Joel Allison: Chairman, Board of Regents, Baylor University

Tracye McDaniel: President, TIP Strategies

Robbie Briggs: CEO, Briggs Freeman Sotheby's International Realty

Hugh Forrest: Chief Programming Officer, South by Southwest

Bill Sandbrook: Chairman, President, and CEO, US Concrete, Inc.

Jeff Cheney: Mayor, City of Frisco

Lorie Medina: Chief of Staff, Mayor Jeff Cheney

Andy Roddick: Chairman, Andy Roddick Foundation

Richard Tagle: CEO, Andy Roddick Foundation

Chris Durovich: CEO, Children's Health

Dolf Berle: CEO, Topgolf

Simon Hjorth: COO, OneAffiniti

Bill Jones: Partner, The Jones Firm

Liana Dunlap: CEO, CoreSpace

Hussain Manjee: CEO, DHD Films

Shezad Manjee: Founder, DHD Films

Amber Allen: CEO, Double A Labs

Mike Rawlings: Former Mayor, City of Dallas

Greg Almond: CEO, Furniture Marketing Group

Brock Purslow: Market Vice President, Humana

Joel Trammell: CEO, Khorus

Carolyn Jenkins: COO, Vericlave

Dan Jones: Vice President, Kubota Tractor Corporation

Masato Yoshikawa: Senior Managing Executive Officer, Kubota Tractor Corporation

David Sutton: President, Kubota Credit Corporation

Darien George: CEO, Mackenzie Eason

Seth Gordon: Principal, Sethica Venture LLC

Tom Montgomery: Managing Partner, Montgomery Capital Advisors

Steve Demetriou: CEO, Jacobs

Gen. Mike Murray: Commanding General, US Army Futures Command

Lt. Col. Patrick Seiber: Retiring Soldier, US Army Futures Command

Nancy Richardson: CEO, San Antonio Shoemakers

Amy Madison: CEO, Pflugerville Community

Development Corporation

Pradeep Saha: CEO, Signature Systems Group

Tom Sanderson: Executive Chairman, Transplace

Nathan Lenahan: Vice President and General Manager, WeWork

Caroline Valentine: CEO, ValentineHR

Paul Sarvadi: Chairman and CEO, Insperity

Clay Gaskamp: Regional Sales Manager, Insperity

Phil Chelf: District Manager, Insperity

Eric Bonugli: District Manager, Insperity

Gary Boyd: Managing Partner, Baker Tilly Virchow Krause, LLP

Zak Everson: Partner, Baker Tilly Virchow Krause, LLP

Beth Garvey: President and CEO, BG Staffing, Inc.

Andreas Schultz: President, Orthopedic Services,
and CFO, Ottobock North America

Eric Salwan: Director of Commercial Business Development,
Firefly Aerospace

Tom Markusic: CEO, Firefly Aerospace

Avi Kahn: CEO, Hilti North America

Ty Harmon: CEO, 2THEDGE

Chris Wallace: CEO, North Texas Commission

Dale Petroskey: CEO, Dallas Regional Chamber

Mike Rollins: CEO, Austin Chamber of Commerce

Paula Gold-Williams: CEO, CPS Energy

Bob Harvey: CEO, Greater Houston Partnership

Jim Hinton: CEO, Baylor Scott & White

Kendra Scott: CEO, Kendra Scott

Harry LaRosiliere: Mayor, City of Plano

John Willding: Partner, Barnes & Thornburg

Kent Newsome: Partner, Greenberg Traurig, LLP

Wade Allen: CEO, Cendea

Pike Powers: CEO, Pike Powers Group

Eddie Reeves: CEO, Reeves Strategy Group

Jeremiah Quarles: CEO, Q Development Partners

Scott Preszler: CEO, US-Analytics

Maher Maso: Principal, Ryan

Sharon Welhouse: Principal, Ryan

Jonas Berntsen: COO, MapsPeople

David Elcock: Chief Diversity Officer, Lynx Technology Partners

Elijah May: CEO, Robotters

Gabe Garza: CEO, Reckon Point

Heather Ladage: Publisher, *Austin Business Journal*

Tracy Merzi: Publisher, *Dallas Business Journal*

Andrew Silverman: CRO, American Airlines Center

Introduction

I wasn't born in Texas, but I got here as fast as I could.

I was born in the Bronx, the northernmost of the five boroughs of New York City. When I was five years old, my parents, Joan and Ed Curtis, moved the family upstate to a town called Greenville—which was quite fitting, as my maternal grandparents' last name was Greene. We were following my grandparents, Mary and John Greene, who'd bought an old farmhouse from farmer Drake for $12,000. It sat on six acres of land, enough for the whole family. My grandfather, whom I called Park (don't ask me why), was a World War II vet who loved his country and family. My grandmother, Mima, was a big part of my upbringing in New York. Within a few short years, their three daughters, including my mother and my aunts Margaret and Marie, had all moved to Greenville. Today, we call it the Compound. I spent my childhood playing baseball in my backyard, running from house to house, and eating whatever food was in anyone's refrigerator. I grew up with my grandparents, aunts, uncles, and cousins. I didn't think I would ever leave.

In the fall of 1990, upon graduating from college, I moved in with my paternal grandmother, Nana, in the Bronx. She lived in a five-story walk-up a short walk away from the bus, which then took me to the 4 train. She spent her entire life in the Bronx, walked to church, and, like many in New York City, never got her driver license. She was a wise woman who eventually passed away at the ripe young age of 104. The first thing I remember her saying to me is, "Listen: you are a country

1

boy. This city will eat you up. So if anyone asks you a question, don't start talking to them. In fact, I want you to get a newspaper every morning. When you sit on the train, I want you to read it. If you don't feel like reading, pretend you're reading it. Do this until you get to New York, and then go straight to the office. Do the same thing on the way home, and I'll see you at 6:00 p.m. sharp." I was to stay with her until I saved up enough money to get an apartment. After eight painstaking months of having to be home on the dime, I was ready to move. I called my brother, and with about $800 dollars in my pocket, I began the journey.

I was twenty-three years old, working in Manhattan, sharing a car, a cat, and a one-bedroom apartment with my brother. We would high-five each other as we crossed paths in our Queens apartment; he had the night shift as a bellman on Columbus Circle, and I had the day shift as a grunt for an advertising agency on Madison Avenue. On week-ends, I would bartend at various watering holes, looking to add to my $14,000 per year job in NYC. My brother needed only one job, as being a bellman was one of the best-paying working-class jobs in the city. We worked ourselves up to the social status needed to afford an apartment in West New York, a city in New Jersey right on the Hudson River. That apartment would be my last stop before heading south. I remember it like it was yesterday.

I was a sales assistant for a media buyer. As buyers, we purchased TV commercial airtime and then brokered the time to clients. The most valued time for a commercial was a thirty-second spot on *The Cosby Show*. My job was to follow up with the TV stations to make sure that the commercial did not only air but met the expected Nielsen ratings. If I put in my time as an assistant, someday I could have the opportunity to be a sales rep. Reps made great money. While stressful at times, the job essentially required that you visit the finest New York City restaurants and use your floor seats to every Knicks and Rangers game, regardless of whether they were last in their conference. Not too shabby. I admired the reps, not necessarily for their lifestyle (though I did fancy that) but for the hard work they had to put in to get to the position. It was a long game with a very steep income curve. And they weathered the storm. To this day, I still believe that if you can make it there, you can make it anywhere. But for me, that meant I was going to be broke for a while.

I didn't like the job that much, and honestly, I wasn't very good at it. It was very repetitive. Same thing day in and day out. What I remember vividly was that I did not envy the big boss in the office. Not for his stature—I envied that—but for his quality of life. He lived on Long Island (where everyone aspired to live) and took the train into NYC every day at 5:00 a.m. Then he had the same commute to get back home after dinner at around 8:00 p.m.—or after the Rangers game at midnight. This was also something my father did from upstate, and it was not anything I was interested in doing for the long term.

Then something happened. I was assigned a new TV station: KTVT, out of Dallas, Texas. I had to get familiar with the station rep who would deliver my information to me. In my job, at least, the business was rather impersonal. The call was usually quick. "Ed here. Did our commercial run? Great, give me the time and ratings. Thank you." On to the next call. But today was different. I wasn't expecting anything other than the ho-hum, "Did it run?" Instead, the rep on the other line said to me, "Nice to meet you, Ed. How is your day going?" After twenty-six years, I don't remember exactly what I said, but it went something like, ". . . What?" And it didn't stop there. The sales assistant, the account rep, and, yes, even the station manager were all the nicest people to talk to. It was by far my favorite account.

Then one day, as we were chatting, she asked me, "Have y'all ever been to Texas?" At first, I was asking myself whether there was someone else on the line. Then I realized *y'all* meant just me.

"No," I told her. "Never."

"Well," she said, "y'all should come down and visit." Again, I was confused: Should I bring a guest, then? All kidding aside, it was at that point that I decided that maybe I should check out Texas. I scheduled a visit.

But before the visit, I had a plan. The plan was to begin a new career. So I applied to as many schools in Texas as I could. Then I applied for a few jobs, including with Tandy Corporation, one of our clients at the ad agency. The bet I made myself was that if one of two things occurred, I'd move to Texas. If I got accepted to grad school or got a job, I'd move. If I didn't get a job, then I would bartend at night, go to school during the day, and hope to survive.

No one knew of my plan, because, quite honestly, it was crazy. But before I headed out to Texas, I made a visit to my Aunt Margaret. I laid out the plan to her and said, "What do you think?"

She looked at me and said, "Go for it. But don't tell your mother, because she will kill me. This would devastate her. But Eddie, you are destined for more, and if you are not satisfied, you have to chase your dreams."

That was all I needed to hear, especially since it came from my Aunt Margaret, who was the mother hen for everyone in our family. If you had a problem, call Aunt Margaret. She was the most giving person I have ever known.

There were a lot of setbacks along the way, but I persevered. Finally, I walked into my office and quit my job. My entire family thought I had lost my mind.

Chapter 1

Why Are They Coming—and Staying?

The feeling I had when I returned to Dallas after my first visit back to New York hit me like a ton of bricks. The second I saw the green outline of the Bank of America Building from my SunJet Airlines window seat, a sense of peace came over me. It just felt right. Other than my Aunt Madeline, Uncle Sam, and the friend of a coworker in New York, I didn't know a soul in Dallas. Yet it felt like home.

As I write this book twenty-six years later, I still get the same feeling every time I approach DFW (now from my Southwest Airlines seat). It's something that will never go away.

Moving is not easy. In fact, it is among the five most stressful life events, alongside the death of a loved one, divorce, a major illness, and job loss. Quite a list of happiness. On a brighter note, moving is often the result of a life-changing event. And whether by choice or necessity, it is an opportunity to change your life for the better. For me, it was a choice—and yes, in the end, definitely for the better.

I'm writing this book at a time when thousands of people a day are doing what I did twenty-six years ago: moving to Texas. Some are moving of their own volition, many through corporate expansions and relocations. Five years ago, I started a venture that helps new companies integrate into the Texan culture after they've decided to move here. I don't lure them here; I simply help them navigate the state after they have moved.

In these five short years, I've learned a lot about the process they went through, their impressions of Texas, and the challenges they faced in luring employees away from their hometowns. Their reasons for moving were rather consistent: taxes, cost of living, centralized location, and lots and lots of land. But their reasons for *staying* are far more profound. I also learned that they expected a lot and, in the end, got much more than they bargained for. I learned that many of them are the state's best brand ambassadors, having called vendors, clients, family members, and even in-laws to pick up and move to the Lone Star State.

I learned that the culture in Texas is like nowhere else in the world and that its ingenuity has allowed them to flourish in business and personal life. In their words, what I learned is that the miracle of Texas is not our cost of living or our warm weather but our people. It's the way we collaborate and help each other out unconditionally. It's like no other place on earth.

What Is Really Attracting Everyone to Texas?

I wrote this book because this story needs to be told. Here's why.

As a citizen of Texas, I have a personal stake in this game. I want it to remain the special place it is: a welcoming environment wrought by an entrepreneurial spirit and an unwavering pride in our state. I feel this is something other states, and even our country, can benefit from. I don't ever want this spirit to go away. I still wake up every day proud to be a Texan. I'm a native New Yorker, and proud of that too, but I'm blessed to be here. And yes, I have called friends and relatives to join me—and many have, including two most dear to me: my mother and sister.

As a citizen of the world, I feel Texans have an obligation to serve. Listen; Texas is not a utopia. Believe me, it's far from perfect. And yes, it has been blessed with natural resources and with a climate and location that make life a lot easier. But as goes Texas, so goes the nation. And whether you like it or not, Texas is now a haven for global business. And with all of these God-given qualities, I believe without a doubt that it wouldn't be the powerhouse it is today without its welcoming people, who have a little bit of crazy in them in the risk department.

If you are considering moving or relocating your business here, you need to know this. Selfishly, I want you to know so that you don't disappoint me. Unselfishly, you need to know so that you'll have the best chance at success and happiness here and so that you will see the value in being an engaged corporate citizen.

So if all you have to do is be nice, how hard is that? It's actually harder than that. It takes work, and it needs to be a part of your way of life. I realize everyone wants a piece of Texas. The good news is, there's plenty to go around.

I am writing this book because I feel the real story of the Texas miracle has never really been told. At a time when people from all over the world are seeking haven here—a thousand people a day, to be almost exact—I felt there was no better time than now.

I am not writing this book to convince the world to move here. I am writing it to tell you that if you choose to move here, there is a set of principles that have kept Texas a bastion of opportunity. If you're in one of three camps—you are considering a move here, you've recently jumped ship, or you're merely interested in the Texas mystique—you're in for a real treat.

Although you might find it odd that a native New Yorker is writing a book about Texas, third-party validation is always the most authentic form of flattery. To make you feel better, I've added a few other people who feel the same, all of whom had the experience of moving here without knowing what to expect. They came from as far as Japan and as close as Oklahoma.

If you are one of the three camps of people mentioned above, I hope you find this book helpful. If you are considering jumping ship and moving your company to Texas, I hope this book helps you save countless hours and millions of dollars. If you have already loaded up the truck and moved from Beverly (Hills, that is), I wish you a safe landing and a newfound love for your new hometown.

After multiple interviews with people from New York, California, France, Germany, and Japan—Fortune 500 executives, entrepreneurs, and even trailing spouses—you will hear a common theme. Texas is welcoming. Welcoming to everyone. And people want to help you. At first, this is awkward and sometimes freaky if you are from a place where talking to strangers is only for panhandlers or the mentally ill.

If you take anything away from this book, I hope you understand that I am not writing this to convince you to move to Texas. In fact, after reading this book, you might decide it is not the place for you. I am simply writing this book to explain to you that if you are planning on moving here, have recently arrived, or are just interested in the mystique of Texas, the true miracle of Texas is in our people—how we see the world, treat each other, and operate a little differently than other places. It is not a utopia, and its flaws often catch the media's attention. But all in all, in my humble opinion, it should be the model for others to emulate.

If you are actually considering a relocation to Texas, my guess is that these are some of your top reasons: it's much cheaper, it's warm, there are lots of jobs, it's centrally located, and oh, did I mention it's much cheaper? At the same time, you are also probably thinking that we ride horses to work, that everyone is packing heat, and that if you're not a good ol' boy, you will have a hard time fitting in. While some of this holds true, it is the exception rather than the rule. In my twenty-six years here, I still haven't seen horses on the freeway.

Before I wrote this book, I researched several others about Texas. There are lots of books about our history, our politics, our bubblin' crude (oil, that is), and Texas Tea. None hit my heart. This book is about people. People who have moved here, many of whom were responsible for moving thousands along with them. Many had to make tough decisions for their businesses, their own families, and other families who were not necessarily interested in uprooting their lives. All of them learned along the way and now proudly carry the state flag (the only flag that flies at the same height as that of our mother country).

In this book, I've interviewed several individuals who have put a stake in the ground here in Texas. Their stories will hopefully give you helpful hints on how to succeed here, how to plan your move here, and how to transition. These are honest, relatable stories about the mistakes they've made, the misconceptions they had, and the lessons they learned along the way. Hopefully, if your company is asking you to come with them, this book will help you in your decision-making.

If you are in one of these groups, you are not alone. As I said before, nearly a thousand people move here every day, many in search of the same thing that I was looking for: an opportunity. In many cases, that opportunity happens to be a job. You might not be sure what that opportunity looks like, but you'll know it when you see it. Regardless of whether you came here by choice or necessity, there are a few things you need to know about this quirky place.

If you are moving your company here, you are likely looking to capitalize on our vast economy. You are also probably looking to hire talented and dedicated workers to help you achieve new heights. If you are moving here because your company asked you to, you might be asking yourself, *Is this really a good opportunity for me?* And if you are just interested in the mystique of Texas, I hope you tell your friends that you read a cool book about Texas and that we are not as crazy as you thought after all.

Texas is a place of people who want to get things done. From entry-level employees to corporate CEOs, there is something in the water that makes everyone feel motivated. It's honestly part of why my six reasons play out. If you don't have that fire in your belly and are waiting for someone to help you figure things out, my six principles probably won't apply. Again, this is why you need to know this before moving here. Step up, or it might not work out for you.

Most important, there is a shared sense of pride among all of us that we are in it together. This, in my opinion, is the most endearing quality of the Texan culture, and I hope it comes through in this book. For me, it was very strange when I first experienced it. In my opinion, losing it could break the Texas miracle.

You might be saying, "That's great, but why do you care, and why are you writing this book?" My answer, ironically, is that I am doing so out of frustration—frustration from living in a place that is comfortable being misunderstood. Texans don't care what other people think, not in an arrogant way (that, of course, is another misunderstanding) but because they are comfortable in their own skin. For native Texans, that might work. For a native New Yorker who cherishes everything special about Texas, it bothers me, in a trivial way.

I've boiled Texas's appeal down to six reasons why you will never leave and, in short order, will be calling your friends and clients to get down here. You might be moving here to capitalize on our rich natural resources, plentiful jobs, low cost of living, and relatively good weather, but these are the reasons why you will stay.

The Six Reasons You Will Never Leave

1. Opportunity
2. Independence
3. Quality of Living
4. Cost of Life
5. Family
6. Pride

Opportunity: Isn't That All Anyone Could Ask For?

In my humble opinion, the real reason individuals and companies are moving here is for an opportunity. The United States was termed the Land of Opportunity long ago. Many of those who came here decided to stay and wrote home to encourage their relatives to make the journey. People began to pour into this land, creating the melting pot that it is today. Today, this is happening in Texas—and in similar fashion. When people began to flock to the US hundreds of years ago, many didn't know why. All they knew was they'd heard it provided opportunity for each according to their ability or achievement. It was an opportunity to make something for themselves—something no one could take from them.

Many seeking haven here are doing so in similar fashion. I know this because I talk to them every day. I live in northwest Austin, and most of my neighbors are from the East Coast, the West Coast, or the Midwest. Because of my profession, I grill them (over casual conversation, of course) as to how and why they chose to move not only to Texas but to the Austin area. Believe it or not, almost all of them had no plan or idea. They'd just heard it was nice and cheap. That's it.

When dealing with large corporations, I find the same. It's thankfully not as simple as for the individual, but not far from it.

If you are an individual, the opportunity you are seeking is likely employment. If you are a budding entrepreneur, it's an environment in which you can innovate and sell to a market willing to buy your invention. If you are a corporation, you are certainly looking to expand your business and hire talented and skilled workers to your team. If any or all of these apply to you, the good news is that opportunities here abound. As with anywhere, they are here if you find them. But they won't find you.

You see, the competition here is different. In big cities, it's a market-share game. Knock on enough doors, and you'll hit your numbers. In big markets, no one really knows anybody, so as long as you have the best price and you bother them enough, you'll probably get a chance. In Texas, it's a game of skill. Here is where the welcoming culture comes into play. It could work against you if you don't understand it. First, you have to care about what you are doing. It's a problem-solving state, so play into that. You might be thinking, *Yeah, that's everywhere these days*, and that's true, but Texas is different. Here, if you are trying to solve a problem that doesn't affect someone personally in any way, they will still help. It's odd, and hard to believe. To this day, I am still amazed when this happens. This goes back to the "getting things done" principle.

After I graduated from the University of Dallas, I was lucky enough to land a job as a temp worker in the loan-processing division of Comerica Bank. My boss came up to me and said, "Tell me about yourself." While I was explaining, he stopped me and said, "Wait a minute, you have an MBA and are working as a temp in our loan-processing department?" I said yes and that I actually felt lucky to be here. He quickly referred me to a woman who was heading up the banking training program, and in a few short months, I was out of processing and into the training program. I was a bit older than the others in the program because banking was my second career at the time. In about eighteen months, I was recruited into a line job as a commercial banker.

To my surprise, I was awarded a healthy portfolio of customers who were borrowing millions of dollars from the bank. I believe this was done by design, because shortly after this came about, my boss said to me that he was leaving the bank to take a position with a start-up bank called Texas Capital. By happenstance, my clients were his clients (that he had passed down to me). My New York instincts kicked in as I realized I hadn't been awarded these clients for my performance but because I was the new kid on the block and would likely lose these accounts to him when he landed at Texas Capital. To this day, he and I are still acquaintances. He is a very nice man and a good banker. I don't blame him for what he did; it's just business. Would have happened anywhere.

What happened next was a complete surprise to me. As I visited each of our customers with my very strong New York accent, the reception I received was extremely welcoming. Keep in mind, comments like, "You're actually nice for a Yankee," did come on occasion, but honestly, it didn't bother me at all. To me, coming from New York, the only compliment that really mattered in business was if they gave me their business. And that is exactly what happened.

As I recall, after I'd met all my clients, I don't believe I lost any of them. While I will give myself a little credit for being sincere in my promise to deliver quality service (and I knew my stuff), Comerica was a quality bank that supported any concessions we needed to make to keep our business. However, banking is no different than other businesses; I'm sure my former boss offered to match my offer.

My point is that I remember what happened to this day. They gave me the business without even knowing who I was or whether I was really going to deliver. They gave me the business because they were willing to give me a chance. I tell this story all the time. I took many life lessons from this. And it actually led to a very rewarding banking career for me.

In conclusion, it is still surprising to me that even as quickly as we are growing in population—and adding more congestion to our streets and resources—our state and city governments and citizens alike continue to say, "Come on down!" All opportunity comes with a cost, but if you understand that you can get yours with a little congeniality (no matter where you are from or what you look like), you will be much better off.

Independence: Deep Down, It's What We All Want

It is a secret formula that does start with a limited-government mentality—that uncomfortable feeling (if you are not from here) that there is no safety net. There is no government that is going to help you figure it out or fix all of your problems. To some extent, that is true. But like any young child that experiences a sense of freedom, it is by far the better alternative—and something that anyone, regardless of their politics, would say makes Texas special.

There are some ancient laws on the books that are making our state have to reexamine itself. But as long as we stick to my six reasons that make Texas truly special, we will be fine. And that is why I am writing this book: to let people know that if you want to be part of a place that you will never want to leave, you just need to know some things that will not wane in Texas. And don't take it from me; take it from the people I was lucky enough to interview for this book.

So if you were wondering whether this book was about why you have to move to Texas, it is not. It is more about why you will never leave Texas—and why you'll call your parents, your customers, your vendors, and maybe even your in-laws to come on down!

Quality of Living: What Does It Really Mean?

Notice that I switched the usual phrase from "quality of life" to "quality of living." I constantly heard that term and wondered what it really meant. So I switched it.

Your quality of living, in the end, really depends on how you want to live. I have many friends and relatives who live and work in New York, and you could never pull them from it. They thrive on the hustle and, honestly, are bored with the niceties of having someone hold the door for them. Believe me, I get it.

When I first arrived in Texas in 1993, I had to do some adjusting. These were the days when you had to walk into the gas station to pay for your gas. Typical protocol in New York is you pump your gas, run into the station (with exact change), walk up to the teller, and say, "Twenty on pump three." Then you hand him a twenty and walk out. I kept doing this over and over again until I started to realize people were staring at me every time. What I never realized is that people were waiting in line to do what I was doing, even if they were just pumping gas. Why would anyone wait in line if they had exact change and didn't need to buy a gallon of milk? While, to this day, I still don't understand, it is only polite to do the right thing and wait your turn.

What makes our major markets so attractive is that they are, in my opinion, the perfect mix between the hustle of NYC and LA without the rudeness. As one interviewer said, in NYC, the waiters make you feel like they are doing you a favor. Here, you still get the hospitality (for the most part). On the flip side, some NYC niceties are lacking here, like tipping. In New York, someone could curse you out, then give you a twenty-dollar tip. Here, they smile and hand you a one-dollar bill. Again, different strokes for different folks. I still like to tip like a New Yorker. Maybe that's why I have a lot of friends.

In Texas, the quality of living is completely under your control. In fact, it was one of the criteria Toyota set in their search for a headquarters in 2014. They were looking to move twenty-eight hundred people to Texas—from California, New York, and Kentucky—and wanted to offer the flexibility of different lifestyles to their employees. I think the lifestyle people are accustomed to in the Bluegrass State might be different than in others. Each of the major metro markets—Dallas, Austin, Houston, and San Antonio—offer country, city, and suburban lifestyles within earshot from many corporate HQs. Again, the city will sleep, unlike NYC and London, but it is a faster pace. When I visited New York, I would always be amazed by watching people with strollers walking the streets after midnight. Where could they possibly be going with an infant at 1:00 a.m.?

So think about what quality of living you want and what your employees want. This is often the number-one reason why it is easy to hire and recruit people to move here. Many Texans take this for granted, often complaining about the thirty-minute commute to work. I just laugh.

Cost of Life: Isn't This Really the Only Cost?

Again, I've switched this from cost of living to cost of life. Sorry, folks; the only cost that really means anything is the overall cost of life. The cost of life is all encompassing. Of course, it includes the tangibles, like housing, electric, gas, benefits, etc.—and, in fact, on their own, many of these are a little more expensive here than in other places. But the cost of life is so much more affordable here in totality. What I mean is that you have to include the intangibles. What is the real cost of sitting in traffic all day? The cost of wear and tear on your car, from salt in the winter to radiator fluid in the summer? Here you can afford a new car, where in other states you just can't. Our energy and fuel costs are some of the lowest in the country, which frees up more money to do other things.

As I mentioned earlier, having family here doesn't require you to drive or fly across country to see them. To this day, we still make several trips to see family. I wouldn't trade that money for anything in the world, but a short drive to dinner with a relative for Memorial Day would save me lots of money.

For businesses, the regulations alone create enough savings to allow you to invest in other places. This allows you to reinvest in your business or give back to the community. Later in this book, I expand on how businesses are very free to give time, money, or expertise to the community to help solve problems, which I believe is because they don't have the expenses they would incur in other markets. This is where culture comes in. Yes, some hoard their money to buy back their own stock. But in general, most are more giving to their local communities and their state than others. Yes, it's a bit territorial—but isn't that what you want from your corporate citizens?

Due to our centralized location, business trips are less expensive because you do not have to fly across the country. In many cases, because so many businesses are relocating here, you don't have to travel at all. The bottom line is that you have to factor in the intangibles. If you do, you will find the cost of life extremely beneficial.

Family: You'll Never Know the Importance of It Until It's Gone

One thing I envy about most Texans is their close proximity to family. I feel this is another advantage Texans have. No one leaves. The kids might go off to school, but they always come back—eventually. In my many interviews, I found that many executives moved to Texas because their spouses required that they do so—to be closer to family.

I made the sacrifice to leave my family to move to Texas. It was one of the hardest things I've had to do, and to this day, it's the only regret I have. Luckily for me, my mother and sister moved here, which was one of the happiest days of my life. But being away from my extended family—missing reunions, weddings, and the like—made it tough. I say this because now, my kids are first-generation Texans. And while I cannot predict the future, my guess is that their family will stay here, giving them the luxuries that many Texans have. So think about this—and about your family situation—as you plan. The odds are that you will not leave. Trust me. So plan for it many generations ahead.

Pride: An Unbreakable Bond

Ironically, I have found that the people who show the most pride in being Texan are folks like me, not the cowboy you saw on the Marlborough commercials. I have a sense of appreciation for everything about Texas that is special, unique, and quirky. It's not a perfect place, but even with its flaws, the sense of pride in being a Texan outweighs any shortcomings it might have.

And as I look back at the time when I packed my bags and moved here, I realize that this was something that, deep down inside, I was yearning for—and I didn't even know it. And if you are reading this book because of your curiosity about Texas, it is what you are yearning for as well. Everyone wants to be part of a winning team—something bigger than themselves. In many cases, whether it be in sports or in real life, the winning teams who do it right always get the most grief. But deep down inside, they are the envy of the league. And as one of the CEOs I interviewed for this book told me, it is not for everyone. To be on a winning team, you have to have a sense of purpose and desire to really be there. The reason why the team cannot be broken—or will be difficult to break—is that its strength does not rest on one person. There is no "leader" in Texas who bestows that sense of pride in each of us; no politician or oligarch who gives speeches on TV to keep the team in line. We are not playing a game in which we *have* to win, but we do so in order to continue to live the lives we lead—and keep the dream alive. For us, it's Texas first.

PART ONE

Corporate Relocations to Emulate

Chapter 2

Toyota North America: The Perfect Plan

JIM LENTZ

No matter what size company you have, if you are looking to move your company to Texas, take some notes from Toyota. In the four-plus years during which they've had their headquarters in Plano, I have had the chance to get to know their CEO and many of their executive team. One of the first execs I met was a marketing vice president, coincidentally named Steve Curtis, who also moved here from New York. So far, no relation, but I might need to compare our family trees to find out for sure. Everyone on the team is all in for Toyota. From my perspective looking in, I believe the culture is what really makes it the company we all know and love. It is what we all should strive for in our businesses.

Toyota in San Antonio

Toyota is no stranger to Texas. San Antonians experienced the Toyota way when, in the fall of 2003, they broke ground to construct Toyota Motor Manufacturing Texas, Inc. (TMMTX), a new assembly plant for building the second generation of Tundra pickup trucks. Second-generation Tundra production was initially split between Texas and Indiana. The $1 billion–plus Texas plant was a three-year project, with the first Tundras rolling off the line in late 2006. One Toyota executive called the launch of the second-generation Tundra the single biggest and most important launch in Toyota's fifty-year history in the US.

The surge in oil prices in 2008 put significant pressure on sales of the truck, and as a result, Toyota had to shut down TMMTX for a three-month period to reduce inventory of the Tundra. In late 2008, Toyota announced that all Tundra production would be moved to Texas. The announcement effectively preserved the jobs of the workers in Texas. Toyota also decided to move Tacoma productions to Texas, which resulted in the addition of 1,100 workers to support the added production. Today, TMMTX owns and operates a manufacturing and assembly facility producing Tundra full-size and Tacoma midsize pickup trucks. The facility employs more than 3,200 employees, all of them an integral part of the San Antonio community.

I asked Jim Lentz, president of Toyota Motor North America, to elaborate on this experience and why they ultimately chose to consolidate in Texas.

Toyota Headquarters Moves to Plano

We all know how difficult it is to get our own teams to carry our flags. Now imagine a company with thousands of employees. Now imagine asking your employees to pick up and move their families to a state where people ride their horses to work. So while my interview with Jim Lentz had my mouth hanging open half the time, in my opinion, the hard work of building an amazing corporate culture is what set the stage for the company's relocation. That said, what they did to prepare for the move was the key to their success, and it's something you need to pay attention to.

Having relocated nine times in his career, Jim Lentz says, "I kind of understand what it's like to put families in situations like this." Jim has done just about everything with Toyota. He started as a line manager in Portland, Oregon, and worked there for roughly seven years before moving to the national headquarters in Torrance, California. From there, Toyota took Jim to San Francisco and then Baltimore. He made roughly three moves back to the headquarters during these stints. Jim took the helm as CEO in 2013. His last move was when he decided to move the company to Texas.

"Portland was a great place to raise a family," said Jim. "All of our kids were born up there. It did rain about seven months out of the year. Baltimore was really interesting. Our kids were relatively young then. They really had a chance to learn about US history. San Francisco was a fun place, and the weather was fantastic. All in all, they were great places to live and will be great memories for our family."

Jim's decision to move the company was more than just a relocation; it was a restructuring of their affiliates in North America. These consisted of a number of separate corporations reporting to different parts of the world, all leading back to Japan.

Manufacturing oversight was in Kentucky. They had a sales group in Southern California with several affiliate companies located in different parts of the US. When Jim dug in, what he really realized was that in today's environment, the most important things were transparency and the development of their team. "I really realized that we had to get everyone together in one location to be able to do a better job," said Jim. He also realized that California does a pretty good job of demonizing Texas, so when they decided to move to Texas, he knew that they were going to have to spend a significant amount of time educating their staff. "We knew all this going in, so we were able to give them a significant amount of time to make their decision on a relocation," said Jim.

"We also had to really examine the culture of each of our affiliate companies and their departments," said Jim. The culture of their sales organization was different from that of their engineering team—partly,

I would imagine, because of their job duties, but also because some were located in California, some in New York, and others in Kentucky. I'm not a world traveler, but my hunch is that Kentucky's work-life balance might be a bit different than New York's. Jim saw the need to plan for what the blended culture was going to be like.

The company didn't lack data, but due to being spread out in different time zones, it was hampered when it came to making quick decisions. Jim saw the need for that to change, as innovation was paramount to the success in the new age of mobility. "In today's business environment, it is all about agility, speed, and the sharing of information," said Jim. "If we did not do something quickly, we could have trouble innovating. We are a Kaizen company: 'no best, only better,'" said Jim. "Being able to innovate was a critical component in our decision."

Toyota has exemplified this strategy of innovation in Texas, working with local universities and hiring at least a thousand Texans after moving here. Coincidentally, the day after our interview, Jim was the keynote speaker for the Dallas Regional Chamber's annual meeting, "The Future of Mobility." Toyota is a leader among automakers, suppliers, and tech companies in patent filings related to autonomous vehicles. While much research is going into autonomous vehicles, cars can provide a lot of data: how they accelerate or brake, when to replace the tires, etc. All of this data can be downloaded to create a more connected car, giving your car the ability to interact with your everyday life. Toyota is also working on technology that connects with infrastructure through radio-wave technology.

In an interview with a local Dallas station, Jim referred to this level of technological intelligence—cars with sensors that will provide driver assistance using information about the driving environment—as SAE level two automation. According to Jim, Toyota is focused on what they call guardian mode, a highly advanced driver support system being developed to amplify human control of the vehicle rather than replace it. There is much advancement in this area, but one thing I will say is that Toyota will be leading—and we are lucky to have them here.

The Plan

The year 2013 was when Toyota began deciding where to move. They started with the top one hundred metro markets, then set a list of criteria they were seeking in a destination and started eliminating locations based on a few nonstarters. First, they felt it would be difficult to relocate people from California to the Snowbelt. They also eliminated locations where they were already headquartered. "I wanted to find neutral ground, and in the end, it seemed to work out for us. By the end of 2013, we'd narrowed it down to four locations," said Jim

In early 2014, they began spending one week in each city to help them make their final decision. This process included eleven people, with eight attending the final trip. One of those eight was Jim's wife, Barbara. Jim wanted a perspective from the eyes of a relocating spouse. Respect for people is the Toyota way. Jim said, "When I spoke to Dr. Toyoda, I remember that the one thing he said to me was, 'Make sure you take care of the people who have taken care of Toyota and cannot make the move with you.'" Fortunately for Lentz, that wasn't too many people.

The planning for the move was meticulous. Jim first looked at the way many other automotive companies had relocated their headquarters and studied their processes. He came across some stunning figures. One glaring case study showed an automotive company that gave their employees only a three-month notice. The result was devastating, with the company losing 75 percent of its employees to the move, something Jim said was not uncommon among corporate relocations. What is even more staggering is that of the 25 percent that moved, half ended up eventually leaving the company. Think about the cost of this and how it could affect your company. The company in this example now had to replace countless employees in their new hometown. The cost of hiring is expensive anyway, never mind in a new town. Then, of the 25 percent who actually did move—which the company paid to move—half of those were gone. The costs of not planning properly could bury any company, especially smaller ones.

"We wanted to keep our team informed, so we basically told everyone in the company, 'If you want a job, you have a job,'" said Jim. Jim said that he wanted them to have as much time as possible to understand the move and to gather the information necessary to make the right decision for their families, for their careers, and for everything else. The company made the announcement in 2014, and within about three or four months, they'd started flying team members and their spouses or significant others to the Dallas area to spend long weekends there. They visited neighborhoods, schools, and churches so that when it became time for them to decide, they had a full understanding of their decision. The average team member had almost three years to decide. As a result, 72 percent of their team made the move. To this day, very few have left.

That 72 percent move rate was no accident. The move itself was very strategic and, in my opinion, a major factor in their success. What the company decided to do was to move the team in waves. Each wave would then build on the successes of the prior, and so on. With this plan, it was essential that the first wave be the driver for the remaining waves.

Jim was part of the first wave. In his words, "If I'd showed up in three years and asked everyone how the move was, that wouldn't have gone over too well."

Those in the first wave—a total of fifty-eight—were called the pioneers. Their office was in a temporary location while the permanent site was being built. During this time, the pioneers worked on the reorganization of the affiliated companies. In 2015, the second wave, consisting of five hundred employees, started moving. Two years later, in 2017, another thousand moved to Plano. The company moved a total of twenty-eight hundred employees.

The Integration

Jim has lived in many places, but he grew up in Michigan, and he told me that in many respects, Texas has the same values as the Midwest. When moving employees to a strange place like Texas, one of the criteria they set was to consider the impact of uprooting families. Giving them choices as to where to live was important. One of the things that made Plano attractive was that it was a location that would give employees the option to live in the suburbs, uptown, in the city, or by the lake. The quality of the schools was also critical. They wanted people to be comfortable with the school systems. Jim remembers asking employees what the number-one thing they liked most about the move was. The answer was the neighborhoods and schools. One of the most memorable responses Jim received was from an employee with younger teenagers who said, "Our kids can ride their bikes in the neighborhood, and I don't need to worry about them."

"I never would've thought of that," said Jim. Jim's kids are thirty-six and thirty-one. A safe community where the kids could go was very important.

Jim also recalled a dealer telling him not to be surprised if his neighbors knocked on his door with cookies or a pie. "It's kind of how this place is. You become part of the community here. You don't become part of a housing development somewhere. It truly has that sense of community," said Jim.

Jim shared a personal example that wasn't surprising to me, but it certainly hit home. He relished in the fact that every year, his wife receives over twenty birthday cards and flowers from local businesses, including her dentist, the florist, and just neighboring vendors. "Not that California didn't do that, but this takes it to a different level," said Lentz. "We were welcomed very quickly at all levels."

Eric Booth, senior manager of communications at Toyota, was on the call for our interview. Eric moved here recently from Cypress, California. He has a young family; his kids are eight and ten. Eric said the schools in California were good, but in Frisco, they have more of a private-school feel. He said the teachers are very engaged and know him on a personal level. "Even after a year of living here, they still ask us how the transition is going. They even remember where we came from," said Eric. Another game-changing factor for Eric was the commute times. When working in Irvine, he had a long commute, often missing dinners with the family and time with the kids. "Now I live ten minutes away from the office, so playing hoops with my kids after work is a real treat," said Eric. He attributes this to the affordable cost of housing in close proximity to work. For some at Toyota, having to find an affordable home led to long commute times of up to two hours. Finally, Eric points out that air travel is a breeze. "The ability to travel and be anywhere in the US in three hours makes it easier to get back home," said Eric.

I realize these are simple reasons that we hear all the time: low cost of living, housing, commute times. But think about how much more productive you or your employees could be if you were living in these conditions. It is a major factor when determining the overall cost of doing business. When we hear "cost of doing business," we immediately think of tangible costs such as taxes, regulations, and the like. These are major costs, but the costs of your people, of turnover, and of unproductivity are likely your most expensive line items.

Below are the criteria Toyota considered when evaluating their move. They broke the criteria down into two categories (team members and company), but some could easily overlap (such as tax benefits, as there is no state income tax in Texas). This information was provided by Toyota management and is presented in no particular order.

Team Members

- K–12 public education
- Livability
- Natural-disaster risk
- Top-fifty university locale
- Climate
- Commute times
- Public transportation

Company

- Ease of doing business
- Projected growth
- Wages
- Office space
- HQ sites
- Diversity
- College grads
- Japanese speakers
- Time zone
- Major airline hubs
- Tax benefits/incentives

When Toyota started looking at locations, they put together an elaborate scoring system. They scored everything under the sun, and work-life balance came high on the list. In writing this book, I determined this to be the most profound quality of this company: their concern for their people. "The advice I would give others seeking a relocation is to seriously ask your employees what is most important to them. If you don't do this, uprooting to go somewhere that is not a fit for your company, its values, and its employees' needs could be a significant setback for your company," said Jim.

I asked Jim what surprised people about Texas after the move. He said politics. The Dallas metro has a mix of everyone from all walks of the political spectrum. The biggest challenge he saw was the weather. "The first year, temperatures of more than a hundred degrees were a shock. As you're here, you adapt. Torrance had great weather," said Jim. One thing Jim said that I found funny was that, early on, the team was nervous about tornados—so much so that they built corridors underground. Coming from earthquake country, I found this rather interesting. I guess that's what they call the fear of the unknown.

Philanthropy

What I find the most revealing about Toyota is the way they give back to the community. In total, company employees are involved in twenty-six local boards, mostly of nonprofits. As Jim put it, their strategy with regard to giving back to the community is threefold: they give money, time, and expertise. He feels the real value a company can give is their expertise.

Upon arrival in Texas, the company decided to utilize the efficiency experts in their assembly plants to work with other nonprofits to help them run more efficiently. The North Texas Food Bank, for example, was a recipient of their help. The food bank was having issues with long wait times for food. After a couple of months, the Toyota experts helped cut wait times down to fourteen minutes. Now, they sit on the board of the food bank to make sure they keep to these standards.

Toyota experts also helped with Hurricane Harvey in Houston. Through the St. Bernard Project, the company sent a team to help cut rebuilding times in half. They also assisted with insurance claims and with increasing the results of collections. By working with local hospitals, they helped these hospitals to reduce wait times in the ER, some of which had previously had wait times as long as four to six hours due to limited availability of rooms. They made a few small changes to improve that process.

Every year, Dallas hosts a holiday parade. It has been a tradition for years. One year, the major sponsor backed out. Toyota came to the rescue and saved the parade with a sponsorship. Toyota gave Collin County a $1 million grant to provide transportation and mobility for the elderly. In addition, they are working with SMU on educational STEM programs with elementary schools. As Jim put it, don't think about just writing a check. Get your employees involved. Consider that third step, and use the expertise within your tool kit to help others. "All I can say is that the environment here makes you feel an obligation to become a part of the community," said Jim. "When I look at Toyota, the reason the move was a success is that our values match. Not every company operates that way. And honestly, if you don't want to be involved, Texas might not be the place to move."

I asked Jim whether he'd made any mistakes along the way. He said, "The only mistake I made was not doing this ten years earlier. But we weren't ready for it. Our timing was just right."

Chapter 3

Corvalent: How a Movie Changed Everything

Ed Trevis

"Life is a lot longer in Texas." That's the reaction I got from Ed Trevis when I assailed him with questions about why he loves Texas. Ed relocated his technology company from Silicon Valley to Cedar Park to save his company from the regulations and high costs of doing business in the Golden State. That's why he came. Ed's reference to an extended life was an extemporaneous comment he made when we talked about his family and about Corvalent's culture now that it's a Texas-based company. It's the reason he is staying.

Ed is probably the most prideful Texan I interviewed for this book. He grew up in Brazil but has stated that the American culture resides in places that you would never imagine. Growing up, he'd heard about it, but living it was a different story. "The true American culture, the culture I came here for when I first immigrated to this country, is in Texas. It's not just a cliché. Anybody can contest me on that," said Ed. He was encouraged by how people valued each other and by the fact that contrary to popular belief, it's Texas first and party second.

But Ed's journey to Texas was not a breeze. In fact, it's amazing he ever made it happen. When he first proposed the idea of relocating the company to his employees, nearly no one wanted to go—and there were fifty of them. What the employees didn't know was that the future of the company depended on it. What Ed did to convince his team to move took guts, a lot of research, and, in the end, an eye-opening exercise that flipped the mind-set of the entire company. Believe it or not, it was a movie that changed everything.

The Story about Corvalent

The story about Corvalent's relocation to Texas is one for the record books. When I first met Ed, he was passionate and full of energy. One thing that stood out to me was how much he cared about his people. That's all he talked about—that and his Vistage group. We were doing research on companies that had been making a significant impact in Texas since they relocated headquarters here. Our work was in partnership with Governor Rick Perry's Small Business Forum held in San Antonio. Governor Perry couldn't make the event, but he sent his congratulations via video.

Corvalent, alongside Topgolf and Lulu's Desserts, ended up winning an award for best place to work for their postrelocation contributions in Texas. Ed's acceptance speech was riveting, bringing tears to many in the audience. Shortly after the event, I asked Ed to sit on my board. He'd always been a friend, even though several years had passed since we'd seen each other. When I thought of writing this book, I knew I had to call him. Luckily for me, he was happy to share his story.

If you truly care about your employees—I mean *truly* care—you will learn a lot from the story of Corvalent. If I'd left out the name of the company in this story, you would have thought it was the story of a Fortune 500 company moving thousands of people. In reality, it was a fifty-person company just looking to make a small mark in the world of technology.

The planning and prognosticating that Ed went through to make the decision to relocate his company is what is remarkable. I'd thought I knew Ed well before this interview, but through it, I learned a lot more.

What I learned is that he is a true visionary. A visionary is someone who does not look at what's in front of them but what is down the road.

Ed saw doom for the future of his company if he didn't move but saw an even bigger disaster if he didn't plan his move properly. If you're going to make the commitment to move your company anywhere, look ahead. Clearly examine what could happen if moving at all proves to be the wrong decision, as well as what could happen if moving isn't done properly. The lesson learned here is to be as transparent as possible. In the end, that is what saved Corvalent—and the families who were committed to its future.

Corvalent's situation was fine. They were profitable, and their employees were working and feeding their families. The problem was that Ed knew that wasn't going to last if things didn't change . . . and soon.

If you are an executive in charge of moving a company, take some lessons from Ed. If you are an employee being asked to move, take note, and open up your mind to the opportunity. It might be the best decision you'll ever make for yourself and your family.

From Silicon Valley to Silicon Hills

In November of 2008, Ed Trevis moved his company from Silicon Valley to a suburb of Austin called Cedar Park. His biggest problem was recruiting talent, and the talent's biggest concern was the cost of living near their job. This difficulty extended far beyond California; trying to lure people from places like Florida and Colorado was even more difficult. In many cases, Ed told me people would even laugh at him on the phone, saying there was no way they were downsizing to a twelve-hundred-square-foot house for a job.

"After a while, I started to think that I could grow only to the capacity of my employee base," said Ed. Ed had a predicament. He either had to find more creative ways to hire or relocate the business to where the talent was. Ed chose the latter.

He started a two-year relocation process, researching eight different states and even considering a neighboring city, San Diego, which had a larger labor pool. The states on the list were Oregon, Texas, Tennessee, North Carolina, Washington, and Arizona.

He quickly eliminated San Diego; while the labor pool was good, the onerous labor laws in California put them out of the running. "I spent lots of money just keeping myself out of trouble, paying lawyers to review our employee manuals, contracts, and employees applications what felt like almost every day," Ed said.

Ed was meticulous in his research. He visited and talked to companies that had relocated to his prospective cities. He then sorted all of his data in a spreadsheet, narrowing it down to the top ten considerations. According to Ed, Texas always met nine or ten; nobody matched Texas. Florida was second, but there were no incentives. The labor pool for tech talent wasn't adequate in Boca Raton, the city Corvalent was considering. Being in the middle of the country gave Texas easier access to more customers all over the United States.

When boiled down, the decision came down to labor pool, government, real estate, weather, access to customers, time zones, and proximity to travel. The only downside in their analysis of Texas was medical insurance. "Initially, we spent more money there, more than in California. But in short order, we fixed it." As you know, the health-care market anywhere is tricky. But Ed looked into options. He met with local leaders and asked them what they were doing. He decided to do something unconventional. He went to a co-op, which is not an insurance plan but a medical sharing plan. This program not only improved their benefits but also ended up being 50 percent less expensive than traditional insurance. Corvalent has had this for a couple of years, and it has been a major success. Corvalent employees are able to put money in HSA accounts, and Ed gives 50 percent of the company's savings back to his employees. Ed learned of this program from networking locally with the president, CEO, and chairman of Goodwill.

Watch What You Ask For; You Might Get It

If you are an employee being asked to move with your company, know that the people in charge of this decision are looking at many factors. In Ed's personal experience, making the move was not an easy thing for him to live with. He had many sleepless nights as he tried to figure out how the move was going to impact people's lives. What if it didn't work? What if the company didn't make it? A lot of people think that CEOs are always thinking about making money via a move. "That is not true, said Ed. "We think about the families, kids, and relatives. It's lonely at the top, especially when we have to make tough decisions like these."

My discussion with Ed hit upon an important question: How would he get his people to have the same gut feeling he had? According to Ed, "If you're doing this just for money, you won't be successful. If you think really hard and do the work, Texas is a great option—from culture to government regulations, weather, the ethics of the people, the culture, the community, etc. Talk about community. Oh my God."

When Ed first talked about relocating the company—to anywhere, never mind Texas—only 5 percent of his people agreed to go with him. At the time, they had fifty employees, which meant fewer than five people would even entertain it, much less commit to it. In Ed's mind, that meant the company was going out of business. He had no idea how he was going to hire enough people that quickly and control everything.

"At that time, there was no way with 5 percent," said Ed. This is where Ed began the execution. He had a lot on the line.

For about eight months, he would fly to Texas every weekend after negotiating with another city. This included a few towns in North Austin: Georgetown, Round Rock, and Cedar Park. Every weekend he would fly with another company family, leaving Silicon Valley at 5:00 p.m. Friday to get to Austin-Bergstrom Airport at midnight. On Saturday morning, they would have breakfast and go to the Bullock Texas State History Museum, which had an IMAX movie that showed a complete picture of what it is to be a Texan. The movie was titled *Texas: The Big Picture*. It talked about where the first electronics chip was invented in Texas. It talked about NASA in Houston, who helped put man on the moon. It talked about Texas energy; it talked about the culture of the state, its people, and what they stand for. After his employees watched this, it all started to make sense. "A lot of people have a negative perception of Texas. When I walked into a room of Silicon Valley CEOs, they all looked at me like, 'Texas? Are you kidding me?'"

They would also look at houses and schools. On Sunday, they would go from school to school so people would have an understanding of their options. On Monday, they would be back in the office in California at nine o'clock.

The Execution

When delivering the message to his employees, Ed had a well thought out plan. He gave a presentation with lots of data, as he wanted to give his employees enough information to discuss the decision with their families.

In July of 2008—six months before the move—he came before his employees and gave them roughly one week to discuss whether they wanted to relocate and to apply with HR. He had no idea what was going to happen. For about two or three days, he thought his whole project was going to go down as a huge failure. Three days later, the director of HR walked into his office and said, "You're not going to believe this, but over seventy percent of the people want to move to Texas."

Ed couldn't believe it. He'd done so well explaining the benefits of moving that he'd created another problem for himself: he couldn't bring everybody. For a lot of people, it had taken seeing it to believe it. He'd had to turn his employees into believers—and now he had to be an influencer and sell them on the idea. Ed's method was simple: send the first wave of people to become ambassadors for the rest. "It had to be based on other people's opinions, not just mine. I spent a lot of time and money making sure," said Ed.

In his own heart, he knew deep down inside that these people were going to have better lives. He reaffirmed to himself that if they didn't like it, they could always move. Since then, not a single family in Corvalent has moved back to California. Ed went with his gut and pushed forward. When I asked how long it took him to realize the success, he said, "About two years. It took me about two years to get that confirmation."

But there was one glaring moment that he would never forget—not ever. A twenty-two year veteran of Corvalent walked into his office to give him some news. He knew that she used to live in low-income housing back in California. She made seventeen dollars an hour and had a child.

"She came to my office one day and said, 'You're not going to believe this, Ed, but I just bought a house!'" I could tell this was an intense moment for Ed. He said, "That was one of the most important days for me. I said to myself, 'We did it.'"

In California, she'd been paying $1,800 a month for low-income housing. Now, she was able to build a beautiful home that today has a lot of equity. Story after story after story. In the end, of the 75 percent who'd wanted to come with them, Corvalent had room for only 50 percent. Having started at 5 percent, he'd had no idea he would overreach the 50 percent he could afford. When some of those people realized they couldn't move, some came anyway. "They said, 'If we move ourselves, would you hire us?' I said absolutely."

A Network of More Than 250 Good Friends

When moving to Texas, Ed had no apprehension about it at all. He felt good about it the first day. After a while, things started getting obvious to Ed. He'd known a little about Texas prior to the move through trade shows and customers, but once he'd started to dig in, he made an interesting comment to me. "I said to myself, 'Oh my God, no wonder what happened here in the last fifty years happened," said Ed. He continued to tell me that while no place is perfect, this place is pretty close. He went with his gut feeling, even though he had a difficult time transferring it to his people at first. The only way he could do so was to show them. "To be honest with you, it was absolutely beyond my expectations," said Ed.

Ed always knew the quality of life was good, but he had no idea he was going to make, in his words, more than 250 good friends. He can count on his hands how many friends he had in California. He said Texans give a new definition to acquaintance. If he ever needed to talk about anything, he could pick up the phone, call a friend, and have lunch.

At first, his family had some apprehension. At the time, his two children were teenagers, and they initially had no interest in coming to Texas. His oldest was ready to go to college. His daughter had gotten into four universities in California as well as the University of Texas (or, as we call it, UT). She'd planned school visits with Berkeley, Cal Poly, and UT. His daughter came back to Ed a month later and said, "Dad, I made my decision." At this point, Ed knew his girl would be gone.

"I'm going to UT," she said. Ed couldn't believe it. He asked why. "I don't know," she said. "I had a really good feeling in my heart that that's where I wanted to be." This meant a lot because she'd grown up in Silicon Valley, where most young kids dream of going. If you ask his kids today whether they would ever live in California again, they would say no. According to Ed, they didn't have that many friends in California. Here, they are so busy with so many things. In the end, he attributes this to the culture and the weather. Ed then made a comment that struck me: "Life is a lot longer in Texas."

Ed noticed that people are more genuine and philanthropic here—and that means more than just writing a check. Here, you participate. "I cannot tell you how much; we don't have enough time. I'm a lot more philanthropic here than I ever was in California, a lot more involved." Though California was philanthropic, in Texas, Ed found philanthropy everywhere. Corvalent is involved with issues involving veterans, local Samaritan hospitals, the Boys & Girls Clubs, Rotary, the Chamber of Commerce, Goodwill, and Meals on Wheels. Ed just finished his seventh year of dedication as a chamber board member. "It's contagious. You do it because other people do it," said Ed.

The movie Ed showed his employees opened up their minds to this concept. "It's a transformational experience when you move to Texas. You earn your right to be a Texan."

Corvalent's Transition

Ed and I talked about innovation in Texas. In the last ten years, Corvalent has transitioned from strictly hardware to a full-solutions company that includes software solutions. The resources, local expertise, and intellectual property they have found here in Austin have allowed them to be more innovative. Would they have done it in California? They would likely have tried, but would they have had the resources to do it? I doubt it. Not in the way that they have here. "It's very different," said Ed. "It was extremely hard to get people to work for you in California. It was too competitive, too expensive, and nobody wanted to move there. It was difficult to grow your competitive advantage. Innovation is here, and there's a lot of money following it now too. I've given people tours of Texas—and would be happy to give you one too!"

Corvalent's Twenty-Five-Year Anniversary

One week after I finished my interview with Ed, he invited me to his company's twenty-fifth anniversary (the company's tenth year in Texas) at the Twin Creeks Country Club in Cedar Park. I've known Ed's story for years, and I knew how much his people meant to him, but this party was special. First of all, it was called a Hats and Boots Party. Before the party, Ed had all of his staff fitted for white Stetson hats. The mayor, the former mayor, the city manager, and the legendary Phil Brewer, the retired economic-development director who'd recruited him to Texas, were all there to celebrate with him and his team.

During the reception, Ed stopped to say a few words and began thanking his employees, his neighbors, and his sister, Liz, who works side by side with him at Corvalent. He told his story about moving to Texas and how it had changed his life. He shared personal stories as he went around the room, telling everyone how welcome they had made him feel.

What impressed me the most was when he gave out achievement awards to his staff based on how long they'd been with the company. There were tears and laughter as he reeled off a long list of employees of this small tech company. Honestly, that blew me away.

Advice from Ed

When I asked Ed what advice, knowing what he knows today, he would give to someone, he said he would say that he should have moved here a long time ago. His recommendation is to talk to other companies who have made the move. Also, make sure all of your key stakeholders are in line with your vision, because you're going to need a lot of help. CEOs do not typically make decisions on money only. You need to know that.

Chapter 4

Ottobock: The Men in Black Coats

ANDREAS SCHULTZ

Col. Steve Austin was the bionic man. With superhuman strength and electronic implants, he starred on the hit series *The Six Million Dollar Man* as one of the most memorable TV characters of the 1970s. He was employed as a secret agent by a fictional government office called the OSI. If you watch the show now, it will make you realize how advanced we have become in cinematography.

Today, if you were to go to the headquarters of Ottobock in, of all places, Austin, Texas, you would see mannequins displaying prosthetic and orthopedic devices that resemble what Steve Austin used fifty years ago in Hollywood. Believe it or not, Ottobock is working on technology that, by using various sensors and microprocessors integrated into the prostheses, can also control the person's prosthetic device, delivering the vital impulses needed to create a bionic-like component. This will make you realize how advanced we have become in technology—and how we can now make a fictional TV character come to life.

To augment its technological prowess, the city of Austin is now becoming a hub of medical technology through companies like Ottobock and Hanger, who are advancing mobility and intuitive control in upper- and lower-limb prostheses. Both companies relocated to Texas—Hanger in 2010 from Bethesda, Maryland, and Ottobock in 2014 from Minneapolis, Minnesota. Their reasons: talent and innovation.

Ottobock

Ottobock is a German prosthetics company founded in Berlin in 1919 by prosthetist Otto Bock, its namesake. It was created in response to the large number of injured veterans of World War I, marking the beginning of a new industry.

In 2014, after basing the US headquarters in Minneapolis for fifty-five years, the company moved to Austin, Texas. As Ottobock looked to the future, they chose Austin for its regional expertise in technology and for its environment, where they felt their employees could flourish. They were looking to grow the organization near a talented workforce that could advance their clinical excellence.

The story of Ottobock's relocation to Texas had both a domestic element and an international one. Domestically, the relocation was challenging because it was the first time in its fifty-five-year history in Minnesota that the company had moved. Unlike in California, where residents might be more accustomed to moving, folks in Minnesota are not. It's a unique culture that has a more conservative mind-set and long family histories of staying in the region. For this reason, the move itself faced unexpected events—events that Ottobock overcame. Today, the company and their people are in great shape. There are some lessons in this move that will prove very valuable to you in your transition.

The international transition involved integrating the German culture of the mother ship and of the person in charge of the transition, Andreas Schultz. The unique combination of these two elements makes the Ottobock story one you can learn from—and a success story Austin can be proud of.

A German Turned Texan

I met Andreas through an introduction from a friend who used to work at the Austin Chamber of Commerce. Since that time, I've gotten to know Andreas quite well. I've been to his house to play German drinking games, and I've spent time with his family during the holidays. I consider him a very good friend. Just so you know, when you drink with a German, under no circumstances should you take a sip before a friendly cheer with direct eye contact. What I didn't know was that this applies to every drink, not just the first. So when an Irishman and a German spend some time catching up, that can lead to lots of glass clinking.

Andreas is a German citizen and holds a US green card. The first time he came to Texas was in 2004. At that time, he worked for Dow Chemical as an international transfer. "The first time I got the cultural shock, the Texas cultural shock, was when I came to Houston from Zürich," said Andreas. He had to switch to a totally different mind-set. He'd grown up in a small village, so Houston seemed like an entire country to him. He was set in his routine, even having to go to the same dry cleaner. As he stated, "I was a small-town boy in a big city. So I guess, in a way, I had to build my village."

Houston, the Center of the World

Andreas had gone to school at the University of Chicago, so he was familiar with US culture. He was a single guy when he came to Houston. He found the city scene was very accepting, welcoming, and easy to connect to. He remembers a time when he walked into a party with a basketball player and, because of that, met tons of people. That was a turning point.

Houston grew on him more and more. "Houston grew to be the center of the world to me," said Andreas. He felt like the world was his oyster. Everyone was approachable, even the mayor.

At first, when Andreas was asked to move to Houston, he was hesitant to make the move. He enjoyed living in Zürich. His boss made it
clear to him that he should be jumping up and down for this opportunity, but it was going to be hard on him. He made the move solo as
a single thirty-seven-year-old, leaving his family back in Germany. He
was alone. In later years, Andreas met his future wife in Houston, and
they got married and had a baby. After two years in Houston, he had
to move to Michigan, the headquarters of Dow Chemical. After a short
stint at the headquarters, he moved back to Zürich with his wife, a native
Houstonian, and his kids.

He had been back in Switzerland for two years before he switched
employers and joined Ottobock, who sent him to Minneapolis. "I wasn't
happy to move back to the US. But in the US, life is much easier, so I
knew it was the right move," said Andreas. As Andreas put it, he spent
four winters in Minneapolis. Then the owner of Ottobock decided that a
move out of Minneapolis was on the table. But the move wasn't going to
be conventional. They decided to move the manufacturing facilities to
Salt Lake City, the warehouse to Kentucky, and the regional headquarters to a separate location, someplace where it would be easier to attract
talent. They agreed that the South would be their best bet. So Andreas
got the order to figure out where to go and to present his ideas to the
owner in Germany. Andreas, who was also the CFO, wanted a low-cost
environment. They also wanted a smaller city than Minneapolis. In the
end, it came down to two markets: Nashville and Austin. Denver was a
consideration, but it was too large for their liking.

From Minneapolis to Austin

After much due diligence, Andreas and the Ottobock leadership team
in Germany agreed on Austin rather than Nashville. It boiled down to

a few things: the vibe, the talent, and the incentives. Andreas visited Nashville—his first time in the city. He felt the pace was slower and that the city had not progressed. The suburbia was beautiful, but nothing was going on downtown. The Austin downtown area was lively and had a highly dense population. He just thought Austin had more natural beauty. "Even though we weren't moving or living downtown, it was much more vibrant. It reminded me more of a European city," said Andreas.

The talent pool in Austin was a major factor. Ottobock is a leader in the med-tech space—medical technology, where health care and technology collide. The company employs more than 650 people in North America and more than 7,300 globally and is the largest provider of upper- and lower-limb prostheses in the world. In addition, they provide advanced orthotics products that help with improving mobility, injury prevention, and rehabilitation. With mannequins positioned around the open-space floor plan in white, their headquarters is a sight to see. You could eat off the floor.

One of their largest customers, Hanger, had also relocated to Austin years prior. This also played into Ottobock's decision. With the new Dell Seton Medical Center in Austin and the Central Texas region's commitment to med tech, Ottobock is in the middle of a slew of talent flooding the area. Texas's technology pool, in software development and the like, is also no mystery. That speaks for itself.

Andreas commented that he was wrong to calculate lower wages, because that has changed. Demand for talent is so high. Of course, he noted that Texas has no state income tax, which is a huge advantage. Other than that, he said wages are pretty normal, like anywhere else.

The last factor under consideration was the financial incentive offered by each city. The incentives were roughly about the same. In the end, however, they didn't pan out—a lesson we will delve into further in this chapter.

The Move

All in all, Ottobock had roughly ninety-five jobs slated to move to Texas. In the end, they offered sixty jobs, and twenty-seven people accepted the offer to move. As a benchmark, Andreas thought that was good. But there was one unexpected factor that caused some not to be able to move with the company: divorce. This took him by surprise. Many employees were in situations in which if they left, they would lose visitation rights to their kids. Because of this, some of those who wanted to move could not.

"I would have loved to have known that earlier," said Andreas. Not that he would've changed anything, but at least he could've been prepared for it. If you are looking to move employees, you need to consider this. Andreas found that some people that he thought he could count on could not move because of this. During the planning process, he found himself looking at his people differently. "'Is he going to come? Is she going to make it?' Or you say, 'Oh, he's not coming.' But sometimes you get surprised."

As with some of our other stories, announcing a move always requires carefully planning regarding the timing. Andreas wondered whether everything would fall apart after he made the announcement. Outside of those with personal family issues, almost no one said they would not move to Texas. Andreas said there was one person who said no because she was afraid of cockroaches. Ironically, though, she's moving to Austin this year, as she has a great career and is moving up with the company. But yes, everything is bigger in Texas—even the cockroaches.

What caught my attention in Andreas's story was his clear memory of the day he told his staff about the move. The situation was personal to him, I could tell. He hadn't known what to expect. He's an engineer by trade, so he was analyzing everything. What if they freaked out? What if they shot up the place? He needed a plan, and indeed, he executed it. Maybe it was a little unorthodox, but it got the job done. But as he told the story, I could tell it had left a mark on him that will live on forever.

The Announcement

"We told them on January 6," said Andreas. The plan was that they would open up a temporary office in May and have the first scouts move in June to build up their outpost. Then they would transition people over the rest of the year. It was more than a year of transitioning. They had a few mishaps, but nothing too major. "I remember that we moved our warehouse over a weekend, which was not smart. That set us back a couple of months. Now that I look back on it, I don't know why we did that," said Andreas.

January 6 was very memorable. It was negative thirty degrees Fahrenheit. "Good timing, I guess," he said with a chuckle. Andreas was happy about the prospect of no more cold weather. He remembers someone suggesting that he get a professional bodyguard in case the announcement set someone off. He was extremely nervous and concerned about safety. "I was thinking, *Great—if somebody makes a stupid move, and we have an aggressive bodyguard who misunderstands the situation, what could happen? What do I know; this is not my country.*"

For Andreas, it was better to be safe than sorry. As Andreas described it, he felt in the moment. There was a bodyguard and a colleague in a long black trench coat. They had guns under their coats. Everybody who walked in saw them. As soon as the announcement started, somebody made a move to get out. The bodyguard followed him. They really expected people would go wild because they had worked at Ottobock for a very long time. But the change was needed, and in the end, it worked out. "It was a tough thing. It was a tremendous help that the owner was there, too, that day."

A Successful Transition

Our first business meeting was when I asked Andreas whether he'd be interested in hosting the mayor of Austin, Steve Adler, at the Ottobock headquarters. He and his team were quite surprised, as attempts to get their mayor in Minnesota had fallen short. Within weeks of a quick call to Mayor Adler, he was there with his larger-than-life smile. He spoke to about a hundred of Ottobock's employees, all of whom were very engaged. It was an easy event to host, as their facility in North Austin is beautiful.

The employees of Ottobock have gone through a positive transformation since their move. Andreas sees a change in the company. Innovation is one of the reasons they chose Austin, as they wanted to connect with the med-tech community. Ottobock is now a medical-technology company in one of the most tech-heavy cities in the country. Recently, Austin has been in the midst of developing a medical Innovation District downtown, so Andreas timed it perfectly. The best evidence of this, as Andreas explained, is that by collaborating with local talent, they have put in place a social-media strategy and an online shop. All of the designers of this initiative are from Austin. "We call them the digital banditos," said Andreas. "They are leading the world in social media for amputees. So if somebody comes to me and asks me why we had to move, I say, 'Go to our web shop, and go to our Instagram. You will know why.' We use it as a channel." Andreas could easily make a business case based on how this alone has made Ottobock more profitable.

Incentives

Andreas's advice is that if you are going for incentives from the state or the city, follow their process diligently. "Don't just go for the money," said Andreas. In their situation, the process of managing the two cities' incentives was difficult. It interfered with business, and the timing of the company's transfer didn't work well with the incentives. In an unfortunate event, someone from Ottobock's PR team told a local publication that they were likely moving to Austin. "As a result, we lost the city incentive," said Andreas. If Ottobock had been relying heavily on this money, it would have been a huge setback. "I learned early on that the incentives cannot be a bottleneck to your operation." In their situation, they had to choose between losing profits or losing the incentives. They gave up the incentives.

In the end, incentives can be a very daunting process and very important to the financial metrics of a move. If you are responsible for this aspect of the transition and don't manage it correctly, you could lose your job. Confidentiality, the timing of when to accept, and the timing of when to announce can be tricky. Plan carefully.

The Future Is Bright

As Andreas looks around his new Texas digs, he thinks about all the people who would not have worked out at Ottobock in Texas. The culture has changed so much, allowing them to prepare for the future. "Our move was absolutely necessary," said Andreas. In Texas, they have fulfilled all of the plans given to them from Germany. A major factor to which Andreas attributes their success is their talent. Austin is attractive to anyone across the globe, and though talent is still scarce everywhere, it's very easy to do a national search, and they found talent much easier to lure to Austin. "People want to move to Austin," said Andreas. "On the other hand, we recently sent two Texas employees to Vienna and Stockholm on long-term work assignments for Ottobock."

For his family, the personal transition has been a success. His kids are enjoying school, and it was very easy for them to connect with classmates because everybody was new. Andreas observed that it was very easy for his employees' families to integrate as well. He knew all of them personally because of the move. "I greeted them, and now their kids are four or five years older. I've seen them evolve." Since the move, some people have gone back to Minnesota, but just a few. Today, fifteen of the original twenty-seven are still here. "Thinking about the time that's passed from my first visit to Houston to today, I realize what a journey it has been. This interview has been a very good experience."

Advice from Andreas

When announcing a move to your team, measure the stress of the situation first. If you don't clearly communicate why you are moving and what your employees' options are, they won't hear anything other than that they must be out of a job. If they are living paycheck to paycheck, that could create some unrest. The customer should not notice any of this, so you need to adjust, and you need to address your employees' unrest quickly. In this situation, Ottobock needed to make that call in February or March, a few months prior to the move. Ottobock hired an HR consultant to deal with the planning. Andreas wanted to move sooner rather than later and felt it was already taking too long, as they had to move manufacturing as well. Of course, this was more than what they'd originally planned. However, in hindsight, Andreas is very happy with the move. "We would not have been able to go through the development we have in the last few years had we stayed," said Andreas.

Chapter 5

CoreSpace: Women Leading in Texas

LIANA DUNLAP

In 2014, I was hosting an event with VisitDallas, then called the Dallas Convention & Visitors Bureau. It was the week after the repeal of the Wright Amendment, a longtime law that was put in place to prevent Love Field Airport from competing with DFW Airport. Gary Kelly, the CEO of Southwest Airlines, came to speak to a roundtable of executives.

I invited a few CEOs who were new to Texas to attend the event. On the invite list was Liana Dunlap, the CEO of a new Texas data center called CoreSpace. Since that event, Liana and I have worked together on several occasions, including meeting with governors Rick Perry and Greg Abbott, the Texas secretary of state, and the mayor of Dallas to discuss business trends in Texas.

Sought-After State for Data-Center Relocations

There are many reasons why data centers seek to relocate to Texas. Data centers are facilities where computing and networking equipment is concentrated for the purpose of collecting, storing, and securing large amounts of data. These centers provide services such as data storage, backup, recovery, data management and networking for businesses of all sizes. Just about every business and government entity needs either its own data center or access to someone else's. Some build and maintain them in house; some rent servers at colocation facilities; and some use public, cloud-based services at hosts like Amazon, Microsoft, Google, and, of course, CoreSpace.

Data centers are coming to Texas in droves. Our electricity costs are some of the lowest in the nation, and with all of the new companies setting up shop in the Lone Star State, the demand is certainly here.

Texas has one of the lowest electricity costs in the country. This alone can save data centers millions of dollars, as they need to function twenty-four hours a day, seven days a week. Texas is the only of our forty-eight contiguous states that has a stand-alone electricity grid within its state border. A nonprofit organization (subject to the oversight of the state legislature and the Public Utility Commission of Texas) called ERCOT is responsible for 90 percent of the electricity in the state of Texas. Due to a deregulated structure, power rates (including renewable electricity) are some of the lowest in the country. This means Texas produces its own electricity and is therefore not subject to the Federal Power Act, a federal commission that oversees all interstate electricity sales. I don't know the numbers on this, but anything with "federal" and "commission" in the name is sure to be expensive.

In addition, multiple carriers' long-haul fiber networks are taking hold in the state, connecting some of the major regions of Texas and the world. Facebook, for example, is building a $1 billion data center at the Alliance Center in Fort Worth, which has dedicated more than four hundred acres specifically for data centers. Throw in some tax incentives for high-volume centers, and you have a ripe market for newcomers.

CoreSpace Arrives in Texas

In 2012, Liana decided she wanted to leave Los Angeles and invest in her own data center outside of California. Her goal was to expand her existing business, relocate headquarters, and purchase a facility. Liana wanted to own a data center and grow it in a high-density market. It is a twenty-four-seven business that often has her competitors leasing space.

Liana was a longtime IT professional who relocated with her husband and kids from Simi Valley. She and her husband both grew up in Southern California. Their existing data center was located in downtown Los Angeles. When she started looking at locations, she researched several potential markets: Arizona, California, Texas, and Nevada. She was particularly interested in business- and tax-friendly states. She noticed there was a lot of activity going on in Texas, particularly in the technology and data-center businesses.

After looking for about a year, Liana eventually chose to relocate CoreSpace to Dallas. She boiled it down to three reasons. The first, as I mentioned, was the power rates. Second was the highly trained pool of talent, and third was the deal itself. Liana found a location close to downtown Dallas that included not only a building but a business to acquire. They were all fixed up!

CoreSpace's headquarters is located off of John W. Carpenter Freeway and Mockingbird Lane, in close proximity to downtown Dallas and Love Field Airport. It's a perfect location. CoreSpace was going through a growth transition. In California, they had been renting a small colocation space. Now, they were owners of a thirty-thousand-square-foot building with HVAC, power, and staff. Within the first week, Liana realized they could not manage this remotely. They were going to have to relocate the family to Dallas.

Liana had never really been to Dallas before, other than for a business trip. When she first visited the facility, it was 105 degrees out. That was one of about one hundred days in a row that temperatures reached more than 100 degrees, something common in Texas. Liana commented, "This is hotter than Vegas." When they did move, they knew no one; on the personal side, they were starting from scratch, with no local friends, family, or support system. Their children were two and five years old at the time.

On the business side, they knew nothing about the community. In Liana's words, "We were dealing in unfamiliar territory." They had acquired a new client base, and in the data-center business, when you're holding a client's data, they want to know who you are. They had to get to know their clients, and their clients had to get to know them. The challenge was knowing who was out there and how to get connected.

The only person they knew when they arrived was the attorney who'd helped them land their building and close the deal. When looking for the right place to relocate the family, Liana knew a commute was out of the question. Coming from Los Angeles, she had spent enough time on the 405 and 101 freeways. They wanted to live close to the business. Their attorney helped them map out the community, and they found an apartment.

Choosing a Prime Location

Liana had, as she put it, spent literally a decade of her life on the freeway. Ever since she moved into her first apartment in Dallas, however, she has always been within four or five miles of the facility. CoreSpace is a twenty-four-seven business with staff on site, so close proximity to the facility allows her to be on site in a jiffy if she has to.

CoreSpace acquired the bulk of their staff through the acquisition. They moved only the family and one staff member to Texas, deciding to keep the rest of their existing staff in California to watch over their LA colocation center. That ended up working out really well.

One of the first things Liana noticed was that people in Texas were nice—quite the change from her experience in California. She would go to the market, and people would say hello to her. "And I would say, 'What? Did he just say hello to me?'" laughed Liana. That was a nice surprise.

In regard to business, the community really welcomed them in. They knew it was going to be a lot of work, but their heads were down. "I didn't know where to go to get my hair done, where to go for a doctor, or where to send the kids to school," said Liana. Because of the quick move, they were starting from zero.

Liana lauded how great the area was for kids. Right out of the gate, she and her husband noticed there was so much to do with them. They spent the first year exploring Dallas. They joined almost every club and membership they could, with organizations such as the Perot Museum, the Dallas Zoo, the Dallas Museum of Art, the Dallas Aquarium, and Klyde Warren Park. "We would go quite a bit and still use these today," said Liana. In Simi Valley, there had been nothing other than the Reagan Library. "Everything was at least an hour for a zoo or museum."

Liana has been spending more time with the kids lately. They joke with their kids now because they are growing up Texan. Her eldest daughter keeps saying "y'all." The family moved to an area near Dallas called Highland Park. They paid more to live in this community instead of going to the outskirts, as Highland Park is one of the pricier communities in and around Dallas. The prices in Highland Park are actually close to those in California, but you can get more square footage. Though the area is expensive, the schools are great, and it is close to the data center, which was a big priority. Suburbs like Plano, Frisco, Allen, and Richardson are much more affordable, but the family wanted to be close to the business. Highland Park and their data center are very near downtown, which is the heart of the business community.

Settling In

Liana and her husband are comfortable here, but they still feel like Californians. The area in which they live houses many longtime Texans, so cliques are definitely present. That is beginning to change as the population continues to grow.

Like many other Californians in Texas, they do miss the oceans and the mountains. However—also like many other Californians—they've had some family members follow them.

Professionally, they've done really well with CoreSpace. Running the business here costs far less than in Los Angeles. But starting from scratch made it challenging. "Doing what we've done here has been a major experience," said Liana. Liana had been a career IT professional for companies like IBM, Amgen, and Disney. Quitting her job to start CoreSpace was a leap of faith. As a mother, the uncertainty of starting all over, packing up the kids, and getting on the plane was bittersweet. It was an exciting time because the journey wasn't defined. The outcome was uncertain. Everything they did was on a whole new level for them, and in the end, they were better for it.

It took a little bit longer to get acclimated to the business community. If Liana could give any advice, she would wish to ease any concerns others might have about moving to Texas. Initially, she worried about not fitting in with the cowboy culture, but that turned out to be the beauty of it. As she jokingly mentioned to me, she's always the one to sit next to the guy with the big ten-gallon hat on the airplane heading back to Dallas.

Paying It Forward

Ironically, Liana just sold her house to a family moving to Dallas from New York. Coincidentally, that family was in the exact same place as Liana was seven years ago.

The wife asked, "Where do I go to get my hair done?"

"Just get in, get settled, and use me as a resource," Liana told her. "The schools are amazing—some of the best schools in the country."

Liana had lived everywhere from San Diego to Cupertino and everywhere in between. "It feels different here," said Liana. Like many I've interviewed, she was also surprised at how many people would invite her into their homes. She'd never been offered that before, nor offered it to anyone before. Now, she's turned into a true Texan, offering help to neighbors. "We talk to neighbors. It's weird," said Liana. "I guess now I'm part of it!"

Leverage Your Public Persona

Liana has received a lot of press in Dallas. Prior to this interview, she was featured in a local magazine called *D CEO*. They did a profile on her and her impact as a woman who has been a leader in the technology industry. Since landing in Dallas, she has invested in her own personal growth. In 2017, she became a Platinum Partner of the Tony Robbins organization after a visit he made to Dallas. This is a VIP group of business professionals seeking to expand their horizons. She was able to take a lot of what she learned through that group and share it with her employees, putting some of them through Tony's Business Mastery program.

One particular incident at one of Tony Robbins's events blew her away. There were about twenty-five hundred people in the auditorium. He picked her out of the crowd and asked her, "What's on your dream bucket list?" She answered that she wanted to start a foundation to help organizations like Operation Underground Railroad (OUR). OUR fights the fight against sex trafficking. Trafficking is a horrific and prolific problem plaguing many communities and young people. She had learned of this organization and their mission to rescue children from trafficking and arrest the perpetrators at a previous Tony Robbins event. After she spoke about this dream, the room ignited with a desire to help the cause, and within fifteen minutes, other attendees had raised their hands and spontaneously offered to donate $300,000! Then Tony Robbins personally matched that! As Tony says, "It is in your moments of decision that your destiny is shaped." Deciding to share that personal goal to a room full of strangers resulted in a donation of $600,000 to OUR. If you stand up at a Tony Robbins event, you are definitely stepping out of your comfort zone. And if you do, get ready for big things!

One of the things Robbins teaches is that proximity is power. Getting involved in and participating in groups with other professionals bigger than yourself is good. Learn more, and apply what you learn to your life. In my work with Liana over the years, she and I have spent time doing some big things. We even sat down with former governor Rick Perry shortly before his presidential campaign in 2016 to talk about her transition from California. Her journey in Texas had only just begun.

Women's Support System

"As a professional woman, if you have children, having a support system—whatever that might look like for you—is important," said Liana. She stresses that women should not try to be a superwoman and do everything themselves. Lean on family and friends. Get help with all of the logistics of taking care of your house, your kids, and your business. Get an executive assistant, and don't wear yourself thin. Getting that structure in place is important. It really does take a village.

In her first year in Dallas, she met amazingly strong women. They had structures around them and were all professional. One was an ER doctor at Parkland; another was a business owner. They opened their homes and families up to Liana and helped her get grounded. They were amazingly smart and talented. "I had many women help me, but on the professional side, that really helped," said Liana.

The Future of Technology for Women

Being in the data-center business with a company the size of CoreSpace is difficult. Liana's competitors are Microsoft and Amazon, and it seems that every month another big company moves here to open up another billion-dollar data center. Liana's advice to women about what's happening in the technology sector in Texas is to embrace all of the STEM programs out there. She stressed that technology opportunities are not just in Austin.

Young women: if you can't afford an apartment in Cupertino, you should take a look at Texas. From programming to management and leadership, the world of IT security has numerous opportunities for women. Networking, connecting, a good cost of living—it's all here. With high housing prices and an extremely competitive job market, California can be challenging. "How tech is helping companies protect data is where it's at," she said.

Chapter 6

The Dallas Stars: From the North to the Stars

Jim Lites

Many people don't know this, but the Dallas Stars originated in Minnesota as the Minnesota North Stars. I grew up in Upstate New York, rooting for the New York Rangers, and was faintly familiar with the North Stars. Back then, the Montreal Canadiens owned the NHL, leaving virtually everyone in the dust. The first sporting event I ever cried over was when the Rangers won the 1994 Stanley cup in game seven against the Vancouver Canucks. For a Rangers fan, it was an absolute miracle. It ended the fifty-four year drought that we were reminded of every day in New York.

When we were kids, we would play hockey on Lake Hawthorne near our house, lacing up our skates, rolling up a piece of electrical tape, and hoping that the ice was thick enough to let us finish the game. My brother, sister, cousins, and I would just shoot around with my dad and uncle, pretending to be Phil Esposito or Bobby Orr.

When I moved to Dallas in 1993, the thought of hockey didn't even dawn on me. So the interview I had with Jim Lites, CEO of the Dallas Stars, was a treat for me. Jim was a big part of the process of moving the Stars to Texas.

There are countless takeaways from the story of this relocation that can be helpful to you. If you come from a hockey market, you might want to pay attention to the DFW area. From juniors all the way to the pros, there is plenty of hockey in the area. If you prefer figure skating, there might actually be more opportunities. Throughout the state, there are minor league teams such as Austin's Texas Stars, the San Antonio Rampage, the Fort Worth Brahmas, and several others in Allen, Amarillo, and Corpus Christi.

From a corporate standpoint, the collaborative effort of the city—including professional athletes like Roger Staubach, political officials such as the mayor, and the chamber—all played a major role in selling hockey to the city of Dallas. It seemed to pan out.

Losing to Disney

Jim Lites was a lawyer in Detroit before cutting his teeth with the Detroit Red Wings, a nemesis of the Dallas Stars. At that time, the owner of the Red Wings was Mike Ilitch, who was not only a client of Jim's but also his father-in-law. Jim was married to Ilitch's oldest daughter, who was vice president of marketing at the Little Caesars restaurants that Ilitch owned. Ilitch had a regional chain of about 125 stores, headquartered in Detroit.

Mike bought the Detroit Red Wings, who played out of Joe Louis Arena in Detroit, out of bankruptcy. Hockey wasn't doing great at that time, having twenty-one NHL franchises. Today, there are thirty-one, seven in Canada. Other than the big markets in the US, the sport was struggling. Then, in 1983, after working for Ilitch as an outside lawyer, Jim came in house, helping run the arena and the business side of the enterprise. Over the course of ten years, the Wings had unbelievable success, raising revenues by about tenfold. He ran the concession operations and the television business. Around this time, the Detroit Tigers built and refurbished the historic Fox Theatre in Detroit and fully integrated the sports and entertainment business around the hockey team. After much success in Detroit, Jim was then, in 1993, recruited by the owner of the Minnesota North Stars, Norm Green. It was a strategic move. At the time, Jim was in charge of the expansion committee for the NHL, which was looking for places to recruit.

They had sold expansion franchises to Anaheim and Florida, and in time, the league gave the North Stars the opportunity to move the franchise almost to wherever they wanted. The North Stars owner wanted a franchise in Southern California. At the time, they were arguing with Michael Eisner as to who had the rights to the California franchise. The expansion committee, of which Jim was a part, had to make the decision. The North Stars owner didn't want to go anywhere other than Southern California. In the end, the franchise was awarded to Eisner.

Numbers Don't Lie

The expansion committee did a very intense study on where to put a franchise. They discovered some astounding statistics along the way. Dallas spent the highest number of dollars per capita on sporting events, retail sales, and restaurants. At the time, Dallas only had about four million residents. When Jim was helping Norm sort out the data, those numbers really stood out to him. People were spending a lot of money on finding things to do. And while Dallas didn't have much of a hockey history, it sure had a lot of indicators that it was going to be successful.

What happened next was a surprise to Jim. "I will tell you, what we didn't anticipate was the growth in the market," he said. People were moving here from more traditional hockey markets from the Midwest and cities like Pittsburgh, Detroit, and Chicago. Since the team moved, the city has grown from 4.2 million in 1993 to a population approaching 7.4 million today. In 2018, Dallas–Fort Worth–Arlington was the fastest growing metro area in the US.

The Stars came because they thought it was a market with a lot of disposable income. Jim told me something surprising. He said that, traditionally, good football markets are good for hockey. They both share a similar demographic. So, of course, with Dallas being an unbelievable football market from high school on up, it was an obvious choice. As Dallas is also really friendly from a business-culture perspective, they were able to achieve some pretty good friends in the business community very early on. "We have been able to maintain that through the twenty-five years we've been here," said Jim.

There were some glaring factors, however, and no one was listening to Jim at first. At the time, they had several meetings and phone calls. Jim was biased against several of the potential markets. He thought markets like Milwaukee were too small, kind of Rust Belt. He was in Detroit and one of the original six franchises in the NHL. Jim mentioned that even Detroit was tough because the economy was so bad and the city was in disrepair. With all the infrastructure problems the city had, Jim commends Detroit for turning itself around. That rebuilding didn't exist in the '90s. He thought Cleveland would be difficult, without any of the positive things that Detroit had. Denver was actually the second best of the bunch and, in hindsight, has proved to be a very good hockey market. He just didn't think it had that dynamic cool factor, and quite frankly, he wanted to get out of the snow.

Norm originally set his sights on Southern California but eventually lost out to Disney. Originally, Norm was from Calgary, where he'd run the Flames before buying Minnesota. In the end, Dallas had a building and a good market. It had guys like Roger Staubach trying to push it along and a probusiness government in Mayor Bartlett. Back then, everyone knew Reunion Arena was going to have to be replaced. By the early '90s, a whole bunch of buildings were in the planning stages. The large NHL franchises were building places like the United Center in Chicago, and Boston and Philadelphia were coming out of their original buildings. Multipurpose buildings were in the cards, and Reunion was not such a facility. "It was functionally obsolete the day it was opened," said Lites. Jim's background as an operator was really how he ended up getting the gig, given his experience with Joe Louis Arena and considering that he had also been around for two significant renovations of Madison Square Garden, one in the mid-1980s.

No April Fools

Jim's first look at Dallas was on April 1, 1993. He remembers because it was April Fools' Day, just before the playoffs were to begin. Norm wanted to show him Dallas. "I remember it like it was yesterday," said Jim. He wore a suit for a job he really wanted. He left Detroit in thirty-nine degree weather with sleet and snow. The Tigers were four days away from opening, so he was certainly busy. On the way to the airport in Detroit, he stepped in a puddle that left a white strip of salt on his shoes, which he worked feverishly to remove on the plane. It was just another reminder of why he wanted out of the cold.

When he landed in Dallas for the first time, it was sunny and eighty degrees, kind of a spring day. Jim remembers getting off the plane and saying, "Oh my God, is this beautiful." They didn't even have offices yet. They were starting off in a suite at the Hyatt Regency downtown.

To close the deal with Jim, Norm made a smart move: he set up a meeting with Roger Staubach, former NFL Super Bowl champion, who was probably the most famous person in town at the time. Following Staubach were several other businessmen who said they would throw their weight around to support the team. "Everyone was engaged," said Jim. "So yes, my first taste of Dallas was really positive."

Jim had always wanted out of the snow, and he was tired of scraping the ice off his car and fighting the battle in Detroit. At the time, however, he really had no other intentions. Initially, his role was only to advise Norm on the expansion team committee, but Norm was looking for more.

Moving the Franchise

Jim had to help the North Stars find a new home. In the process, they looked at about seven US cities, including Denver, Colorado; Cleveland, Ohio; Milwaukee, Wisconsin; and, in Texas, Houston and Dallas. Right off the bat, Dallas showed very good potential. After long negotiations with the city, Mr. Green made the decision to relocate the team to Dallas.

"Detroit was great to me," said Jim, reminiscing about his great success there. He is the last guy to knock that city. But after ten years, it was time for him to move on. He and his family had been big advocates for the city, always digging hard to try to put a positive spin on it. They had moved the Little Caesars headquarters downtown and helped renovate a theater. But it was always an uphill slug, and a big part of that was because most people in Detroit were so negative about the city—a clear contrast to Dallas's positive vibe. Everyone was making money and changing the world. "I was always shaken by how positive people were about being from Dallas or from Texas. It sounds kind of corny, but it's so true."

Throughout this process, Norm made it very easy for Jim to consider coming to work for the Stars. The more he learned about Dallas, the more attractive it became to him. Norm gave him a piece of equity and a very solid employment contract to start the franchise in 1993, and that's how Jim Lites got to Dallas. He's had a long run here, with three different owners over the course of twenty-six seasons. He won the Stanley Cup and personally had success on and off the ice. To this day, Jim is very involved here in Dallas. He's a member of the Chamber of Commerce; he got involved in baseball for a three-year stint as president of the Texas Rangers; and he was instrumental in the building of the American Airlines Center and the renovation of the Victory Park area, the largest environmental cleanup project and most dynamic public-private partnership in the sports business.

According to Jim, what the American Airlines Center and the developing area around it have done for the city is almost indescribable. "The National Hockey League knows it made an unbelievably great decision to relocate a franchise here," said Jim. Norm, too, made the right decision in picking Dallas and leaving the Met Center. "Personally," said Jim, "becoming president of the Dallas Stars was the best career decision I've ever made."

Today, Jim's thirty-year-old son is the head of amateur analytics and an amateur scout for the Stars. His wife is a retired Olympic skater who enjoys Texas as well. Jim has four kids here and couldn't be happier. Life is good.

Relocating the Team

The North Stars relocated the entire franchise to Dallas: eighty people, including players, coaches, and staff. The players had to adjust to the weather, which, needless to say, is a bit more mild than Minnesota.

To prepare the team for the transition, Jim had to explain to them what Dallas was like. He jokingly told them, "Dallas is Chicago, just a little more polite." He had to recruit a lot of players here from Canada, Finland, or Sweden. At first, of course, they all thought it was Cow Town. They quickly they came to realize it was a business town with hustle—business vibrancy, they called it, with a Southern feel.

Jim's advice to others would be to come and spend some time here. There are no cattle. "Guys come here and buy ranches," Jim joked, "but they don't ranch. They own ranches for fun, but they don't ranch."

One of the most important—and intelligent—things the state adheres to is that it has no state income tax. After living in Michigan, which had a sizable income tax, Jim immediately felt the difference. High taxes on sales and property lose their importance because of the lack of state income tax, which is felt in your paycheck. Implementing such a tax would be regressive. The lack of it helps psychologically when it comes to making decisions.

Roger Staubach and Don Carter

On countless occasions, you will hear how aggressive the business community in Texas is when it comes to courting new businesses and welcoming them into the state. The same goes for government officials, who are some of the most probusiness in the country.

In this case, three people were instrumental in making the Stars relocation happen. The first was Steve Bartlett, the mayor of Dallas at the time. Steve was very dynamic and did a great job of making Norm feel important. The second was Roger Staubach. Norm had met Roger through a friend from the Naval Academy who happened to own the Hartford Whalers, and he became a good friend to Norm and a confidant. He was very engaged in helping Norm make the decision to relocate. As Jim Lites put it, it really was a community effort.

Ironically, the third—and most important—person who influenced the relocation was the owner of the Mavericks, Don Carter. "Mr. Carter controlled Reunion Arena, and it would've been very easy for him to blackball that decision," said Jim. Coincidentally, that's exactly what happened in Houston. The Rockets controlled the arena there. The owner refused to even talk to the franchise about moving to Houston, which at that time was every bit as big as Dallas in terms of market size. With the success of the Houston Aeros, it also actually had a much more significant hockey history than Dallas. Mr. Carter, to his credit, didn't hesitate. He basically went to the city mayor and said, "No, I'm not necessarily crazy about hockey, but it's good for Dallas, so it's good for me." Jim was always appreciative of that.

In the late '90s, in the middle of the building process, Don Carter sold the arena to the Perots. He did it for the right reasons—and, to his credit, sold to a very significant Dallas business family. By doing so, he ensured that the American Airlines Center would be built. The Stars were also sold in the mid-1990s to Tom Hicks, another significant Dallas businessman. Between the Perots and the Hicks Group, the American Airlines Center became a spectacular arena. It is like no other.

Both Tom Hicks and Ross Perot spared nothing to make the building great. If you build these structures well in the beginning, that means less money spent later. They understood this. With really good architecture and a great location, the center is designed to expand and stay vibrant. "We could be in that location for a hundred years, quite frankly," said Jim. To this day, the Stars share space at the American Airlines Center with the Dallas Mavericks. Before the Mavs were purchased by Mark Cuban, the team endured a well-known losing streak throughout the '90s. Cuban's relentless perfectionism has made the Mavericks great corporate partners and cotenants to the Stars.

Players Stay

Retaining and recruiting talent is at the top of the list for most businesses. The sports business is no different. The Stars, over the years, have had some dynamic players. Minnesota was a traditional hockey market, so players like Neal Broten were gods there. Neal was team captain during the Miracle on Ice at the 1980 Olympics. Minnesota is a great place for hockey, but Neal, along with other players, came to enjoy Dallas for the same reasons we do: the weather, the practice facilities, the cheap real estate, and the lack of state income tax. The team had to overcome the standard preconceived ideas about Texas, but it didn't take them long.

When Jim showed me the long list of players who have moved back to Texas to retire, I couldn't believe my eyes. Marty Turco is one of my favorites. The Stars have an active group of alumni, nearly fifty of whom live in Texas, including Eddie Belfour, Brenden Morrow, and Jason Arnott. A significant number of retired Stars come back. Recruiting players and management is never any trouble. Their only major objection is the heat, and the players don't play then anyway, so most spend the months of July and August vacationing.

Housing and taxes are major appeals to professional hockey players. "A house that would cost $5 or $6 million elsewhere would cost $1.5 million here," said Jim. This is a huge consideration for professional athletes.

The absence of a state income tax is also a major benefit for a professional athlete. In states with income tax, players are taxed for the games they play in that jurisdiction. Cities like Boston, Philly, San Jose, Los Angeles, and Anaheim charge players for the days they play there, including visiting teams. The caps under the new tax code definitely hurt the players in those markets, affecting their deductions. If you play in Texas, you have no state income tax for all home games, so a very small percentage of your overall income goes to state tax. Players in states with income tax are taxed on almost all of their income.

"Playing in Dallas definitely helps these guys because we're in a fully capped league," Jim explained. A player that makes $5 million a year in

Texas would have to be offered $7 million in California or New York for the income to truly be equal. "That plays out when it comes to bidding on free agents, and don't think we don't use it," said Jim. He shows these players how far their dollar will go in Texas.

Third Time's a Charm

In 2007, Jim got let go by Mr. Hicks for the second time. He moved around, working for the New York Giants to build a football stadium in New York and then moving from Dallas to East Rutherford, New Jersey, to build MetLife stadium, working for the Mara family for two and a half years. Shortly after this, the Stars fell into bankruptcy.

One day, the guy that bought the team out of bankruptcy called Jim out of nowhere to pick his brain. After four years, Jim found himself back in his old office, interviewing for a job—he thought. The new owner, Tom Gaglardi, needed to rebuild the team from scratch.

Their meeting has been written about in local newspapers in the past. This is how it went according to Jim.

"Tom is a tough guy, a no-BS kind of guy. He's a really good listener and prober. In my first meeting with him, his first question was, 'How old are you?'

"I told him, 'That's illegal. You can't ask me that.'

"He said, 'I know. It's illegal in Canada too. So how old are you?'

"I was fifty-eight at the time; I'm sixty-six now. His second question was, 'Is this a job interview?'

"I said, 'I don't know.'

"He said, 'OK, let's assume it is. Why the heck would I hire a guy who failed at this twice?'"

Jim's answer was, "It's not my damn fault this company went bankrupt."

Tom's plan to tick off Jim so he would open up worked. This meeting went on for two or three hours. Afterward, Jim called his wife and told her it had been a bust. "Well, honey, it's not going to be a fit." They joked about not quitting their day jobs and still laugh about it to this day.

That night was opening night for the Stars, with the team still under bankruptcy protection; Tom's deal wasn't to close until November. Jim attended a going-away party that night. Tony Tavares, president of the Stars at the creditors' request, came up to Jim and asked him how the meeting went. Jim's response: horrible. Tony said, "No, man, he loved ya!"

Tom Gaglardi visits Texas often, but he lives in Vancouver, where his father started Northland Properties, the largest privately held hospitality club in Canada. They own every Denny's in Canada, as well as hotels and ski resorts. Currently, they've got six projects cooking in Dallas. Their most notable project is Moxie's, the most successful franchise downtown.

Tom might live a thousand miles away, but these days, Jim has a closer relationship with him than he's had with any other owner. He talks to him literally every day, and they've had really good success rebuilding the team—which has been good for the franchise as well as for the city, quite frankly. "It's been seven years, and I absolutely love the guy," said Jim.

A Good Corporate Citizen

Today, the Stars franchise is very engaged with local executives. The team put together an advisory board that includes many people who moved companies here or moved here to run companies. These include Joe DePinto, the CEO of 7-Eleven; Tom Greco, who was the CEO at Frito-Lay; and Avi Kahn, the CEO of Hilti.

All of these executives look at the area in the same way. They share the mind-set that we're all in this together. The city pulled together in similar fashion to recruit Amazon. What's really amazing is how welcoming Texas is to new ideas. The people here figure out how to make things work.

The Impact of Hockey in Texas

Coincidentally, as Jim and I were conducting our interview, Dallas had just finished hosting the largest youth hockey tournament in Texas history the past weekend, consisting of 187 teams. As we talked, Jim looked out over the rink. When I moved to Dallas, there was one ice rink in the city. Now there are twenty-five. In 1993, a total of 120 kids played here—all ages. Now, that number is in the thousands.

So if your kids play hockey, know that the youth programs here are unbelievable. Another astounding fact I learned in my interview with Jim is that there are more registered figure skaters in Dallas–Fort Worth than anywhere else in the US. Why? Because there is so much government participation in building ice rinks. Jim knows because the Stars operate them.

The suburbs of Dallas are investing in rinks as an amenity for their communities and to accommodate people moving here from cities like Chicago and Boston. Now, there are rinks all over town in McKinney, Plano, Richardson, and Farmers Branch, to name a few. Forty percent of these figure skaters are of Asian heritage. There is a significant Asian community in Dallas, primarily Korean and Chinese.

Innovating in Texas

The Stars have the most dynamic franchise in the NHL when it comes to partnering with local communities to build ice rinks. When Jim was in Detroit, the city had sixty sheets of ice, so they never needed to build. After his franchise bought their first rink in Dallas in 1993, they haven't stopped building since. The Stars have built or bought twenty-two; the most any other franchise has done is four. "Giving is part of the community here in Dallas," said Jim

In buying the Stars from Hicks, the new group also negotiated the purchase of the Texas Stars minor league team in Austin, which included the rights to their arena. Who would have thought there would be an American Hockey League (AHL) team in Austin, Texas? But there were several reasons to buy this team. Firstly, as Jim put it, it's good to control your AHL team. They also had an agreement to put their players there. Furthermore, it came with seventeen acres of developable land. Since then, they've ended up buying twenty-five contiguous acres adjacent to it. Now, the biggest Apple installation outside of Silicon Valley sits six miles away from their site, so the investment has certainly paid off for the group. The Texas Stars are actually one of the best franchises in the AHL. Go figure!

Jim also recently negotiated the naming rights of their Frisco facility, formerly known as Dr Pepper Arena, to Comerica Bank. The Texas Legends, the G League team of the Dallas Mavericks, are also tenants of the building.

Jim has had a twenty-year relationship with Comerica, which used to be the National Bank of Detroit. They also used to bank with Little Caesars. In the early '90s, Jim sold Comerica the naming rights to the stadium of the Detroit Tigers. Since then, the Comerica headquarters has also relocated to Dallas. Now, Comerica is a lead banker for the Dallas Stars franchise and has the naming rights to their training center in Frisco. How things come around.

Chapter 7

CytoBioscience: San Antonio, Leading in Biotech

JIM GARVIN

"I'll tell you right now: if I had to bet where a cure for cancer will come from, it will come out of the state of Texas."

That's Jim Garvin's take on the biotech industry in our state. Jim is the CEO of CytoBioscience, a biotech company that relocated to San Antonio in 2016.

"There is already stuff happening right now with a company in San Antonio run by a woman who has made major breakthroughs in lung cancer," Jim said when I interviewed him for this book. "She's this close to being able to cure it."

That should give you an idea of how this dedicated man feels about his home of less than four years. However, although Jim wasn't born in Texas, his father was, and one of his relatives, John Garvin, was one of the immortal thirty-three at the Alamo. So Jim does have some Texas roots. Even if he didn't, though, I'm guessing he'd be in the right place.

But back to biotech. Texas isn't exactly the first place many think of in that context. Silicon Valley in California? Massachusetts? Sure. But Texas? Jim moved to San Antonio as a result of the acquisition of a biotech company out of Germany called CytoBioscience, formerly known as Cytocentrics. At the time, the company was looking for a new home. In their search, they discovered some interesting facts about San Antonio they hadn't previously known.

For instance, they learned that there were more than ninety thousand biotech jobs in Texas, putting the state at number two in the country for jobs in biotechnology. (Connecticut is number one.) Texas has more biotech jobs than California or Massachusetts and also leads the country for PhDs in biotechnology across the board. One out of every six jobs in San Antonio is in biotechnology and health care. San Antonio boasts one of the largest concentrations of the health-care industry in the United States. Within fifty miles of the CytoBioscience corporate headquarters lie thirty-five hundred biotech companies. I bet you didn't know that either!

In Jim's words, "It's an extraordinary and wonderful place."

That doesn't mean he doesn't get frustrated with both Texas and San Antonio. He's frustrated that the biotech industry is undersold in Texas, taking a backseat to other favorite industries, such as manufacturing. The presence of Toyota and the influence of the San Antonio Manufacturers Association in the region make that industry a tough act to follow. And from a city standpoint, San Antonio doubtless takes a backseat to the more aggressive areas of Dallas and Houston.

According to Jim, cities like San Marcos, Houston, Dallas, and Fort Worth all have a lot going on in biotechnology. Yet he feels we treat ourselves as if we're the stepchildren of the country.

"We are the leader. We are number one," he insists. "It's not like we have to think about how to become number one or whether we should go out and seek to be number one. We *are* number one."

In other words, Texas is where everything is going on if you're in biotech. It's a great place to be and a rich, diverse, robust, and dynamic business community.

Jim is seventy-one and has lived all over the world, but he believes Texas is where you should be wanting to do business—one of the best places in the United States to do business, hands down, no question. "And if you're not happy in Texas, trust me: you're not going to be happy any place else."

Who Is Jim Garvin?

Jim was very fortunate. No one in his family had finished high school, but when he was fourteen, a teacher said to his father, "Why don't you let your son stay with us so he can finish school?" His dad thought that was a good idea, so he did. Jim ended up being a pretty good student. He graduated, got a scholarship, and went to college as a philosophy major. He ended up getting his PhD in economics instead. He never did get to be a philosopher.

Jim is the oldest of fourteen children. His childhood was much different than his life today. The whole family consisted of crop workers. They would pick cotton in Oklahoma and Texas, then go west to California to pick various fruits, then up to Washington and Oregon to pick apples, then straight to the Midwest to pick corn and, finally, back down to Oklahoma in the winter. Then they would do the whole thing all over again.

He went to Texas for college in 1965 and left in 1967, not to return again until 2015. Before Texas, he resided in Florida, Alabama, New Mexico, Colorado, California, Washington, DC, and London. But Jim does not intend to move anymore.

He did not know he was going to end up in Texas. The company thought they were going to go someplace in Canada or Florida. But a group of guys in Texas encouraged them to come look here. "Once we began to dig into what is going on in Texas, I said we'd be idiots to go anyplace else," said Garvin.

Why San Antonio?

More than one consideration drew Cytocentrics to San Antonio. Texas was not the only state they looked at that had no state income tax; however, when they put all the pieces together, it just made sense for them.

One attractive quality was that the state government was very vocal about wanting to get businesses here. In addition, the culture in San Antonio is more diverse than most know. There's a deep German presence in cities like Fredericksburg. If you pay attention, you'll notice that several streets in San Antonio bear German names. "So, you're getting this wonderful Latin, Hispanic, and Mexican culture that's woven throughout the state with wonderful French and German influences. It's a wonderful tapestry that you can feel the fabric of, and it's really pretty cool," said Jim.

Jim did not relocate many employees with the company headquarters. He and his wife made the move with two folks from Germany. Once they arrived, they hired from within the state. Their moving experience was extremely positive. Jim has traveled the world and lived in many places, but Texas was the most welcoming place he'd ever been. People wanted to talk with him and find out about his life. Jim hasn't experienced other markets in Texas, but he said it would be tough for them to hold a candle to San Antonio.

Cytocentrics received a fair amount of press coverage when they arrived in San Antonio, so that certainly got him attention. But what surprised him was his ability to network with people outside of the biotech industry. Neighbors invited him to play golf; even his doctor introduced him to people who had the same interests as him. "It's a very communal place," said Jim.

The Search

Cytocentrics researched for about six months before choosing San Antonio. Other locations considered included Florida and Canada. Canada offered significantly more than Texas—*significantly*. But the cold weather there and the overwhelming benefits Texas offered meant it wasn't enough. Florida is warm, has no state income tax, and offered a lot more money. When it comes to why San Antonio ultimately won out, the biotech industry played a major role. "We started thinking, 'Gosh, why would we want to be anywhere else?'" said Jim. The combination of no state income tax, a great culture, and warm and friendly people was overwhelming, in a positive way. "The more you peeled back the layers of the onion, the more you went, 'This is a no brainer.'"

The Florida lifestyle was different. It was more expensive and involved a lot of traffic. In San Antonio, his commute to work was twelve minutes. "One complaint I would have about San Antonio is that we need a bigger and better airport," joked Jim. "You just can't get there from here." The places he needed to go did not offer many direct flights to San Antonio; every once in a while, he would get a direct flight, but often, he still had to go through Dallas or Houston.

Curing Cancer in Texas

CytoBioscience focuses on finding cures for things that are killing people, such as brain cancer, breast cancer, cardiac issues, and Alzheimer's. CytoBioscience considers it their responsibility to advance medicine for the good of the people. Jim's job is not necessarily to find a cure for cancer but to make sure they find a way for people to get better faster. To this end, CytoBioscience has forged a collaborative relationship with the University of Texas Health Science Center. In addition, the

Center for Innovative Drug Discovery has exponentially expanded their capabilities.

The Future for Texas

Jim is very bullish on Texas, but he understands that it will be tough to keep our residents employed, educated, and healthy as our economy changes. Jim used Boeing as an example. Boeing makes a lot of tiny parts for it's airplanes, and if you walk into a warehouse in Seattle, you'll find about three thousand 3-D printers making these parts. No people, no sick pay, no overtime, no vacation—just self-operating printers cranking out parts. "The world is going to change rapidly in front of us because of the things happening in technology," said Jim.

Texas can't look at the thing that's right in front of them: automation. "If I were Texas, I would pour everything I could, everything I could, into technology," said Jim. He wasn't partial just to biotechnology; whether biotechnology, robotics, or artificial intelligence, he would jump in as hard as he could. He thinks that doing so will ensure that there will be places for people to work in Texas. "The ground is not going to shift under you," said Jim. He also alluded to the fact that Texas needs to make sure that we have an education system that drives people toward these industries and prepares them to work in these fields.

Many of the needed positions in his industry don't necessarily require a PhD or even a college degree; what you might need is two years of college and strong technical training. "In biotech, you can always go out and hire a PhD, but really good lab techs are hard to find. We either to shoot too low or too high" This applies to anywhere in the US, even in Massachusetts or California. Jim would focus on technology and on an education system that feeds into that.

Texas Leads in Health Care

San Antonio is also a leader in Texas health care. In fact, when the MD Anderson Cancer Center was being put together, it was in San Antonio, not Houston. Furthermore, when the Walter Reed facility moved out of Washington, DC, it moved to Texas. When it comes to the health-care facilities in Texas, he feels that "the state needs to embrace them and grow the dickens out of them."

He can't believe that people will get on an airplane and go to the Cleveland Clinic for heart treatment when some of the best cardiologists are right here in the state of Texas. "Recently retired Steven Baily at Dell Medical School was one of the best-recognized cardiologists in the world. Quit thinking that we're not good enough," said Jim. "We're the best; embrace that. Texas really has a lot going for it, but that has to come from the top, from the governor on down."

Texas should do everything it can to drive technology, not just in biotechnology but also in transportation, distribution, printing, lighting, and communications. "Across the board, embrace it, and get ahead of the curve," said Jim. "People chasing Amazon for this new headquarters right now is great, but I'm gonna tell you something: all those jobs are going to be replaced by robots. All of them. Who's going to build the robot? The only people building robots right now are the Koreans and the Japanese. It needs to be us. I think, despite the politics, the intertwined feeder system needs to be in place in case it were to become a priority."

Raising Capital in Texas—or Not

One of Jim's only knocks on Texas is the ability to raise capital here. "Texans like to invest either in oil or someplace else," said Jim. The biotech community at large raises money outside of Texas. Many go to

New York or San Francisco because that's where they can get funding. He would like to see more local investors look at investing in biotechnology. "Many support the med school, but if you're looking for a group of people to work with start-ups and help bring them along, you're not going to find that. Alabama does a much better job with that than Texas does. In the last seven years, Alabama has led out of their innovation depot in Birmingham. It's easy to give somebody $1 million, but they're going to burn through that, and where do they get the next $2 million?" More often than not and time after time after time, people get start-up capital, but the fund that gave them that capital does not know how to go out and get the next round. "Texas is not the only state that suffers from that."

At age seventy-one, Garvin is ready to retire soon. He plans on staying involved with the business as a consultant, though. "I love what we do. I love this company, and I love the people, but we're public. In public markets, they always want to know there is some young eager beaver at the helm. I'm gonna help that young eager beaver go out and knock 'em dead."

Advice from Jim

There's a lot you need to do to prepare for a move. First, find out whether the state and local governments are supportive of your business and your industry. That ends up being more impactful than people might realize. Second, make sure you understand the housing market. There are some places in Texas where the market is pretty brisk and housing is not that cheap. Austin is a perfect example. There was a time where housing was affordable there; now, it is less so. Housing is very affordable in San Antonio, but cities like Austin and Dallas can be expensive depending on where you're located. Third, people with families in particular need to check out the school system. Texas has good schools—better than a lot of people think.

Both the state colleges and universities in Texas are some of the very best in the country. You don't have to be ashamed of your kid going to Texas State, the University of Houston, St. Mary's, the University of Texas, or A&M. All of these are really good schools.

Before you think about coming to Texas, think about what it would be like to move to Connecticut, New York, Pennsylvania, California, Oregon, Washington, or Nebraska. Then compare what you find out about those places to what you find out about Texas. There's no comparison—just no comparison. Jim has lived in all those places. His advice: don't be afraid to compare; don't be afraid to dig; don't be afraid to look. You'll find that you're going to feel very good about coming to Texas. And lastly, no, you do not have to support the Dallas Cowboys. Jim remains a New Orleans Saints fan.

Chapter 8

Andy Roddick Foundation: Tennis, Anyone?

ANDY RODDICK

I was fortunate enough to interview both Richard Tagle, the CEO of the Andy Roddick Foundation, and Andy Roddick, the chairman and founder. Each of them relocated to Texas on separate occasions and for different reasons. Andy moved to Austin two days after he won the 2003 US Open and relocated his foundation there from Florida soon after. Richard moved to Austin from Washington, DC, and Andy's foundation later recruited him to run it.

Andy Roddick

In 1991, my brother, my father, and I went to the US Open. We were lucky enough to be among the few people who stuck around to watch the infamous Jimmy Connors match during his comeback year. It was a night match against Patrick McEnroe. Jimmy was down 3–0 in the third set when everyone started leaving the stadium to beat the traffic. We, however, stayed all night and watched Jimmy come back to beat McEnroe. Before my interview with Andy, I wondered what he had been doing then. He was nine years old at the time. The US Open is infamous for being in the direct flight path of LaGuardia Airport. Andy told me that while we were watching the match, he was flying over the stadium in one of those annoying planes. He looked down and couldn't believe they were still playing tennis after midnight. Andy ended up spending that whole week sneaking into Jimmy's matches. Since then, Jimmy has become a great friend of Andy's. Andy said with a laugh, "Jimmy doesn't like talking about tennis, so I always make him tell stories about that tournament." I thought that was pretty cool.

I grew up as a huge tennis fan. My father taught my brother, my sister, and me how to play. My brother and father are still very active in the business. My brother, John, was head coach of NYU's men's tennis team from 1996 to 2006 and now owns and operates the Manhattan Tennis Academy in Chelsea, NYC. My dad runs a masters tennis program in the Villages, Florida, and donates all of the revenue from his company, Curtis Tennis, to a local multiple myeloma support group. He's seventy-eight and plays almost every day. My sisters, Jennifer and Janine, and I are just casual players. So my interview with Andy was a treat for the whole family.

For those of you who have been living under a rock and don't know Andy Roddick, he's one of the best US tennis players to ever play the game, having won the US Open in 2003 and once held the coveted ranking of number-one player in the world. In 2014, during a Davis Cup semifinals match, he produced what was then, at 155 mph, the fastest serve in professional tennis. In 2017, he was inducted into the International Tennis Hall of Fame. Andy has a keen knack for business and is someone who is going to do big things for a long while on this earth. He's thirty-six years old and way ahead of his time. Standing on the world stage at age twenty-one will certainly help prepare anyone for what the world will throw at them. Personally, I attribute that to the game of tennis as well. In tennis, your biggest enemy is not your opponent but yourself. And yes, I've beaten myself at tennis many times. For Andy, it's quite the contrary. If you ever see him in an interview, you'll see that he owns the camera. He's sharp and witty, and if he catches you on your heels, watch out. I've seen him do it to commentators, and it's hilarious. He was genuine in our interview, but I hope to see that side of him some day. I have a feeling I will—and I hope I'm prepared.

Andy's History in Austin

Andy Roddick was born in Nebraska and moved to Texas when he was three years old. His dad moved his business to Texas when he was eleven. They then moved to Florida to pursue Andy's tennis career, but in 2003, at the age of twenty-one, he returned to Texas.

Andy's dad was in the Jiffy Lube business in Nebraska and came to Texas to scout locations. One of his stores was on Thirty-Fifth and Guadalupe in Austin, now a well-trafficked intersection. He had a few other locations around town, and during one visit, he bought a house in Austin—without Andy's mom ever seeing it. Andy's dad sold out in the mid-1990s.

"It's funny—I think people still think of Texas as a place where everyone wears cowboy hats and rides horses to work," said Andy. He has certainly seen Austin change since he was a young boy. Even when he moved back in 2003, Austin was kind of one of the better kept secrets in Texas. As Andy put it, it was big enough that you got great concerts, but you never really had to deal with traffic. Austin is a progressive pocket in a state that is not. It's a mix of business and of people who are on different sides of the coin, but it seems to work. "In Austin," Andy said, "more so than in any kind of other place, people are willing to listen."

Austin was always home to Andy. He always knew he was going to move back. "It was just a matter of life sequencing. I won the US Open, and two days later, I flew to Austin and bought a house," said Andy. "It was basically just when I could." He knew where he wanted to live, and it was just a matter of getting there. During his first trip, he flew from New

York to Austin and looked at houses; then he moved in once the season was finished in November. "And that was that."

Relocating the Foundation

What most people don't know about Andy's career is that he actually started his foundation when he was seventeen years old—long before he came into any significant money or fame. The foundation has less to do with tennis and more to do with education. Its focus is on financial literacy and tech literacy in a space that's really underserved. If you look at a picture of something today and one of the same thing seventy years ago side by side, whether it's a business or a geographic location, they'll look totally different. One will be in black and white, one in color. Buildings weren't as tall; the steel mills probably look operationally different. But in school, things have generally remained the same. You still see students in desks, sitting forward. It's one of the only things that hasn't progressed. The Andy Roddick Foundation focuses on out-of-school programs after the school day and during the summer break, as it's in these idle times that there is the biggest divide between the educations of students from higher-income places and those from places that aren't as lucky. "That was a void that we felt we could impact," said Andy.

For a long time, the Andy Roddick Foundation was a pass-through organization. They started in Florida and moved to Texas. But like a lot of other nonprofits, the foundation's strategy was simple: raise a bunch of money, and donate that money to organizations that were doing a good job. "That model is not sustainable once relevancy comes and goes for a while," said Andy. Initially, people would come to his events because he was number one or two in the world in tennis. However, a good friend said to him, "Listen, man, you need to start thinking about how to make this so it's still here in twenty years." So Andy took ownership of his own programs, decided they were going to do it themselves, and put a major focus on the out-of-school time space. The first school they partnered with, which they did in 2014, had some eighty kids. Today, they serve three thousand students daily, making a lasting impact on children throughout the Austin area.

The foundation has become laser focused on after-school programs in a targeted area, Austin, Texas. In Florida, they started with a funding strategy that relied more on personal donations from retired Florida residents. In bad times, funding slowed because these donors were watching their money. In Austin, the idea was to gain donors who believed in the mission and wanted to be a part of a movement. With the massive growth of donors in the corporate world, they could partner with companies with similar missions and really deliver value to the market. The Austin culture aligned well with this plan, and Andy wanted to piggyback off the growing Austin market. Most importantly, he saw that the need was local, meaning that local dollars would be going to solve a local problem. Andy had been taught by a mentor early on that you can't raise money somewhere and take it away. If you're raising money in Austin, Austin should get the credit for what you're trying to build. So when he moved there, the natural progression was that the foundation should be there as well, especially as Andy took on more and more of a leadership role within it.

To make this shift, there were a lot of things they needed to do. The first was proof of concept. The foundation was tackling this out-of-school space not only as something for the kids but also to address a socioeconomic divide. The entire family benefits from such programs. Think about it, even with your own family. If a parent has to leave work early to pick up their children to take them to after-school programs, they often miss work and lose pay. "When these programs are in place, parents can stay longer, get another few hours a day of compensation at work, and better provide for their family—all while their kid is in good hands and not just being babysat," Andy explained.

The foundation started adding value, and once they got buy-in and people understood what the out-of-school space was, things started to roll. They started with one school, then two schools, then three schools, and then they started running different programs for the city's parks and rec department. "That was a huge partnership for us," said Andy, who describes the program as a hybrid model of direct service rather than just giving money away. Partnering with other organizations in Austin created a fast growth path for the foundation. Andy had the ability to explain to people what they were doing. He has really gained the trust of locals here in Austin who will do anything to help him see his vision through. They have a staff on the ground to design programs, execute them, and deal with families. "We've made a lot of really good hires who have done an amazing job."

Building a Stellar Board

A lesson anyone can learn from this chapter, whether the company they're moving to Texas is nonprofit or for profit, is to consider adding a few locals to your board. Andy's foundation has thirteen full-time employees right now, a volunteer base in the hundreds, and around eleven or twelve programs. He attributes much of their success to his board. "Every time we have a board meeting, I get a free education," he said. The board is comprised of entrepreneurs and former executives from Dell who have contributed business expertise to the board and have been instrumental in executing the new strategy of the foundation. Andy admitted that, aside from this foundation, he hasn't built anything from the ground up, so being able to gain knowledge from people who have done that before has been important for his personal growth. "We apply a lot of their practices to the foundation," said Andy, who, once you meet him, is a rather humble guy.

Most of the board members are local, but some are not. Billie Jean King was very instrumental early on. She was a board member that he went to frequently for advice. Having her name supporting the mission was a big plus for the foundation in its formative years. Her support allowed the organization to blossom into a local powerhouse close to the cause. Andy also attributes their recent success to the hiring of Richard Tagle, whom I interview in chapter 9, as CEO. Richard moved from Washington, DC, where he had worked in the nonprofit space for more than twenty years. Andy is clearly happy to have him.

The Future of Austin

I asked Andy what future challenges Austin, as a growing city, will face. "Infrastructure is our biggest challenge. You can't have close to two hundred people moving into the city every day and not deal with problems with roads," said Andy. Fifteen years ago, they didn't have traffic at all, no matter what the time. Budgetary concerns over the growth being so fast are also a reality. So is land. Austin is approaching one million residents. When growth happens that fast, real problems arise. Andy doesn't worry about the spirit of Austin, the business mechanisms, or the downtown area. "Gentrification is going to be a big issue, and I think infrastructure is something that's going to have some growing pains."

The tax structures in Texas can really benefit the younger population. "It's a great place to rent while you're young," he said, as this demographic can avoid property taxes while taking advantage of no state income tax. Furthermore, Austin isn't defined by a predominant industry like oil or banking. Technology is a problem-solving industry that lends itself to collaboration more than most others. Andy lives this approach on a daily basis, collaborating with a variety of technology companies looking to solve educational imbalances in Austin. He's a big networker, always on the circuit. He takes his job seriously.

Networking in Austin

"It's funny, said Andy. "Austin becomes a very small town very quickly when you act in good faith with the companies that are grown here. Kendra Scott is a great friend of ours. What she's accomplished and the valuation that she's attained is incredible. With Kendra, it really revolves more around what we can do for you. She has spoken at events for us, she's given money, and she cohosted our gala last year. She always kind of leans in, especially on Austin-centric initiatives. The focus on the community of people who have made big business here is very giving. You're not calling and talking to someone's secretary. You can call someone and say, 'Here is what I'm thinking; what do you think?' It's a very quick and honest conversation. It doesn't really work like that in other places." Another Austin icon Andy is familiar with is Tiff's Treats, with whom he is an investor. "Tiff and Leon are amazing," said Andy. "They are a huge asset to the Austin community as well."

Why Austin? Spirit, Hard Work, and Low Taxes

When Andy came back to Austin, he was only twenty-one years old. That June, he had broken up with a coach who was based in Florida; the new coach he was working with was in California, but he wasn't moving there. Austin seemed like a more realistic possibility inside of his world of tennis. It had facilities where he could continue to compete. He was growing into an adult and was beginning to get comfortable with life after his first three or four years on tour. This was a place he loved, and it had always been home for him.

For Andy, as for many of the others I've interviewed, the spirit of Texas always feels different. "Here, people want to build toward something, as opposed to going into the viciously protective mode you see in some other places. You don't get a lot of conversations that are kind of stuck in the mud. People outside of the state might think it's arrogance, but I think it's confidence and pride in being Texan and kind of holding that mantle."

Andy is of the mind-set that if you are willing to put the work in, you can make it anywhere with a supportive climate. "I wasn't going to move to Minnesota as a tennis player, but at that point of my life, as I was starting to make decent money, the taxation and the income tax in Texas probably made a lot of sense." He admitted, though, that if he hadn't been from here, he doesn't know whether he would have made the move back as soon as he did. However, he has no regrets. He had an idealistic vision of what moving back to Austin would be like, and it was just what he expected.

Another barrier to coming back would have been if it hadn't been beneficial businesswise. "When I met my wife, she loved Austin, and that was a huge bonus. As far as moving back, it all kind of worked out without a lot of stress. I know that's not always the case, so I feel fortunate it was that way."

Athletes in Texas

I mentioned to Andy that it really does mean a lot to a city when star athletes stay. Such has been the case with David Robinson in San Antonio and Emmitt Smith in Dallas. His response said a lot about these players but also gave some credit to Texas. "David Robinson is obviously not going to have more value anywhere in the world than in San Antonio, with his legacy there. The same goes for Emmitt Smith, so I think that speaks to how Texas embraces athletes and the people who have certainly won for them." Roger Staubach is another example of someone who has done just incredibly crazy things in business on the heels of being a sports icon in Texas. They are all huge assets to our state. "Texas certainly does support their own, and that makes it hard for you to leave—not that you would want to."

Advice from Andy

I asked Andy for advice for anyone, particularly athletes, who might be looking to move to Texas. He didn't know that he had any advice; however, he did chime in with some advice for athletes who are starting out and in the first big earning cycle of their life. Texas is affordable. A lot of his friends live in California, and they all say how expensive it is there. When he moved to Austin in 2003, he wasn't paying even close to what others were for housing. "With all the different business ventures they've been in, they've looked back fifteen years later and said, 'Man, that was probably a pretty good move you made, Andy.'"

I was curious whether any of those other players had impressions of Texas, good or bad. He didn't know whether players on the tour knew too much about Texas. The thing that always surprised guys who came to Austin to train or visit is that they would see the hill country and the lakes and say they'd thought it was going to be flat and full of tumbleweeds. Andy would then tell them, "There are certainly parts of that in West Texas. We do have automobiles and everything here too!"

I had to ask him about Roger Federer, since I knew he had been in town recently. Roger had come to visit and unfortunately was only in Austin for about six hours. Still, Andy was grateful that he'd come, knowing he doesn't have a lot of days to spare with the tour and his business. "We were coming in from downtown Austin. I had picked him up at the airport, and as we drove past the capitol, he said, 'Hey, man, pull over, pull over.' And I was like, 'What do you mean, pull over?' 'You guys, pull over. Let's take a picture in front of the Texas State Capitol.' So I did that and put it on Twitter. I thought that was pretty funny that, with everything that he has seen, he was still interested in taking a picture in front of the capitol building of Texas."

Chapter 9

Andy Roddick Foundation:
A CEO's Move from DC to Austin

RICHARD TAGLE

Richard moved to Austin in June 2013 after twenty-seven years in Washington, DC. Andy recruited him to run the foundation after Andy relocated it from Boca Raton, Florida, to Austin. The foundation had been based in Boca Raton since 2000. For the first twelve years, the foundation was a pass-through organization, basically raising money through tennis matches with 98 percent of the funds going to youth development organizations across the country. When Andy retired, he wanted to come back to Austin, so he brought the foundation with him. His plan was to focus on grant making within the Austin community, and he wanted the foundation to really have legs. Andy was looking for someone who was very well versed and experienced in growing organizations, designing and running programs, and really getting the community engaged in the process of growing the foundation. In 2013, Richard was hired.

What he tells people about his interview is that he was very impressed with Andy, the board, and the staff. At the time, there were only three other people on staff, but they were all remarkable. "That was the first time I met Andy Roddick," said Richard. He'd always seen him on TV and found that how Andy acted in person was exactly the same. If you see him being interviewed on TV, you're not looking at two different people. Here's the athlete, and here's the foundation chair;

they're the same person. He's a very down-to-earth guy, and Richard was impressed with that. He was also very impressed with the board's strategic approach. He saw the board as a group of people smarter than he was. If he were being recruited to be the smartest person in the room, he probably would have stayed in DC. But he was really impressed with the fact that he could learn a lot from this position. He was essentially starting from scratch, and that interested him. The foundation, at the time, didn't have any programs. "It was a fresh start for the foundation, and I wanted to be a part of that."

Removing Preconceived Ideas

"I had a lot of trepidation about relocating," said Richard. "I thought, when I was being interviewed, that the foundation was doing national grant-making work based in Florida." At this point, the foundation had already moved to Texas. So his first thought was that if they were doing national work, perhaps he could do that from anywhere and would not have to move away from DC. When they said that the work was going to be in Austin, he really had to ask himself whether he wanted to leave the city that he'd lived in for twenty-seven years. His impression was that Texas was a very conservative state and that he wouldn't fit in. Washington, DC, is a very liberal city, diverse and metropolitan, so he was very hesitant.

Prior to moving, Richard spent some time in Austin working with nonprofits that operated there. The people he worked with painted a picture of Austin that was quite different from the rest of Texas. "My research showed me that it was like a blueberry amid tomato soup. That started to make Austin palatable for me."

Moving here was a surprise to him. In DC, everyone was labeled by their political affiliation. What Richard noticed in Austin was that, among Republicans and Democrats alike, everyone's mind-set was about how to make the community better, how to make sure that it continued to be better, to grow and develop, and to remain a community where young families could afford to raise their children. "That, to me, was like, 'Yes, this is why I want to live here.'"

He was already connected with people from Austin through national networks, so he was able to reach out to them and ask what it was like to be in Austin. First, he learned it was very casual compared to DC. He liked that idea of not having to wear a suit and tie to work every day. As we spoke, Richard was actually wearing a T-shirt and jeans—pretty much a regular day for him now. Many told him the cost of living would be a lot cheaper in Austin. "It was for the first two years, but that's basically becoming a fallacy now," said Richard. "Things are getting just as pricey in Austin."

Again, he felt that the open mindedness in Austin was unlike anywhere else in Texas; however, he qualified that by noting that he has not been to every place in Texas. "I see that local elected officials and community leaders are open minded about making the city more diverse and global. That distinguishes Austin."

For the first twelve months, he still wondered whether or not he'd made the right choice. It wasn't until about two years later, between his second and third year here, that he really felt that this was truly the place for him. The turning point was realizing that Austin is an open-minded community. "It is very . . . I wouldn't say *liberal*, but it's welcoming of new ideas."

Discovering Austin

Tagle has discovered a lot since he's been here. He's been on the boards of College Forward and, until 2018, the Learn All the Time network.

He's noticed that there are always conversations happening about innovation and all kinds of issues pertaining to the roles of technology and of nonprofit work.

He is keenly aware that there seem to be a lot of eyes on Austin and how the city's development will play out over the next several years. There is a focus on not becoming like Silicon Valley, where everything is so expensive and unaffordable, and a conversation about Austin remaining very friendly while also being very competitive in its advances in technology. He is very connected to this idea. He feels it is important that families have a place where they can raise their children, have access to good schools, and have a home that they can afford.

There are not too many metropolitan places where you can raise a family affordably anymore. While Austin has only about one million residents, many want to start planning now to keep the schools and quality of life intact. "In a sense, we're still at a point where we can address these issues now—as opposed to California ten years ago, when parts of that state had already crossed the bridge of multi-million-dollar homes and high cost of living," said Richard.

I absolutely noticed that Richard was deeply engaged in community issues, specifically ones relating to families and children—for obvious reasons. He follows the discussions around policies and incentives for businesses to transfer here, making sure that there are jobs here and that people can afford to live in the city. One such infrastructure conversation concerns what it would take to keep commute times down. "That is the number-one complaint right now: traffic," said Richard. "It's not yet at the level of San Francisco or Washington, DC, but we can't afford to wait until we've hit that point. Public schools are still performing well in general. There are a lot of improvements to be made, but the school districts and the mayors are collectively discussing how to address them—not just in the city of Austin but in the surrounding areas."

Connecting with Local Issues

If politics or local legislative issues are of interest to you, there are many opportunities to get involved. That is one area that Richard has delved into, not for his job with the foundation but on a personal level. Professional networks in Austin have helped him, particularly an organization called Mission Capital. He also enjoys the Innovation Plus group, which includes venture funders, social entrepreneurs, and start-up leaders. Joining local nonprofit boards has expanded his network and given him a way to learn more about what organizations in the area are doing to address local issues. He went to as many city council board meetings as he could so that he could hear what people were concerned about.

After two years, he realized people were genuine and clear about what they wanted to do, how they wanted to help, and what they wanted to see in the community. "It is like going to a party where you don't know anyone, so you start to mingle and feel out whether or not this is a party of like-minded people or people with different opinions." After a while, he noticed that everybody he met wanted to do good for the community. They were very honest, authentic, and sensitive to how others would be affected by their decisions. They're very concerned about gentrification here and how it pushes low-income families out of the city proper and into the suburbs. They are concerned about what jobs these people would be taking and how this would impact children with high mobility rates. It heartened Richard to discover that people were thinking that way. That's when he realized he wanted to live here. "I don't plan on moving anywhere else."

He pointed out to keep in mind that when he was in DC, he was surrounded by politicians, many of whom were there temporarily. It is a very transient city compared to Austin. Very few people consider DC their home base. They are there for four years, two years, six years, or however long their business there lasts, so when he dealt with people in DC—many of whom he misses—he always wondered, in the back of his head, about their sincerity regarding what they really wanted to do. Were they just there so they could maximize their time in office? Understanding how he approached things in DC helped me understand his perspective.

A Life-Changing Move

Richard lived in Manila until he was about sixteen and a half. He then moved to San Francisco for four and a half years before moving to DC for graduate school. He stayed in DC for almost twenty-seven years and has been in Austin for almost six years now. Of all of his moves, the biggest change he made was from DC to Austin. Moving here from DC wasn't a decision he took lightly. He wanted to be somewhere significant. If he was going to uproot himself after twenty-seven years, he wanted to move to a community he planned on staying in for a while. His move from San Francisco to DC was motivated by graduate school; his move from DC to Austin was to determine where he wanted to spend the rest of his time. He didn't want to be doing this every three years.

"My husband and I are on our twentieth anniversary, so he moved here with me," said Richard. Before, he lived in a thousand-square-foot condo in Newport Circle; now that he is here, they live in a five-bedroom house with a huge backyard and a pool. Richard's husband went to SMU in Dallas, so he was more familiar with Texas than Richard was. He initially had a harder time professionally because he had to step down from UNICEF in DC. While working for UNICEF, he'd commuted from DC to New York on an almost weekly basis, but when they transferred here, he couldn't do his job remotely. He had to step down from his job and look for work here in Austin. It took him about a year to find work, but he's settled now.

Philanthropy in Texas

"I think Austin is just beginning to become more philanthropic," said Tagle. Dallas, Houston, New York, and DC are in a similar vein of having tons of opportunities to raise money. There's a much younger population in Austin, without as much older-generation money as there is in Houston and Dallas. Michael Dell, for example, is a very young guy. All of these venture funds are basically comprised of people in their thirties and forties, so the emerging wealth is very young. Still, there is a lot of this new wealth, and though the economic and philanthropic capacity of Austin hasn't been maximized, it's beginning to get there. As a fundraiser, the question Richard asks himself is: What is this tech-based wealth going to do? He wouldn't be surprised if, ten years from now, they'll be at the same level as Houston or Dallas. "But right now, people are just beginning to understand their capacity to give."

He remembers one meeting he had with an oil company in Dallas, where he was fundraising nationally. After forty-five minutes, they were guaranteed a half-million-dollar grant. Right now, things are not that easy in Austin, but he sees that changing over time.

Advice from Richard

Richard advises that wherever you move, it's good to know the community you're moving to. Really participate and be engaged in community life. Attend as many committee meetings, school board meetings, and city council hearings as possible—anything that would give you an indication of how engaged people are and what kind of issues the community is trying to sell and overcome. Secondly, know your neighbors. Not just those within your neighborhood; know other people who live in other sections of the city. The very few people Richard has met, for example, who live on the west side of the city rarely take time to visit the east side, even for restaurants or other amenities. People seek convenience now. You've got to know the city you live in, not just the perimeter in which you reside.

Texas itself is a very huge state, and these major cities are very big. Some of the smaller cities are much less detached than some of the larger cities. While the larger cities are more diverse than Austin, neighborhoods are much more segregated. Richard lives in a compound where an Indian couple lives next to him, a Korean family lives across from him, and two doors down lives a Chinese family that moved here from Sacramento. He loves that such a diversity of folks lives on his street alone.

Chapter 10

Hilti North America: A Culture of Giving

Avi Kahn

"The degree to which the community is so warm and philanthropic was probably my biggest surprise." That was the answer Avi Kahn, president and CEO of Hilti North America, gave when I asked him what most surprised him about relocating to Texas. Avi's only prior experiences in Texas had been short airport layovers, so he'd never had a chance to really see those qualities firsthand on a daily basis. This was also the top response I received when I posed the same question to other executives in this book. I often wonder why that is so.

But Avi's answer stood out to me for a couple of reasons. First, as it was coming from someone leading one of the most philanthropic companies I've met, this was quite a compliment. Globally, the Hilti name was built on a world-class culture of taking care of employees, bringing innovation to customers, and giving back to the community. It's the bedrock of their brand. The second is how Avi embraced the role once he arrived. If you were to emulate anyone in this book in terms of how to really jump into the scene, Avi is your guy. His personal and corporate commitment to the community is evident. In the short amount of time Avi has been in Dallas, he has embedded himself into the community better than any other. If you are an executive new to Texas, take notes from Avi.

The Story of Hilti

The relocation of Hilti North America's headquarters to Plano really drives home the importance of culture and of aligning the values of your company with those of your city. The company did not stretch too far in their move. In 2015, 250 team members packed their bags from a stone's throw away in Tulsa, Oklahoma. Since that time, Hilti has nearly doubled its number of team members in North Texas to more than 600.

The culture of Hilti begins at its global headquarters in Schaan, Liechtenstein, where the company was founded nearly eighty years ago. Hilti sells products, services, and software into the construction industry, including, among many things, the legendary red tools you see on construction sites.

I initially met Hilti through a connection with their former (now retired) CEO, Cary Evert, a New Jersey native who was instrumental in moving the company to Dallas. This was my first look into the Hilti company, which was impressive from the start.

We dove in headfirst with Hilti, participating in an event called "A Brush With Kindness" (a Habitat for Humanity initiative). The program helped transform neighborhoods by providing critical exterior home repairs, including painting and landscaping. Hilti provided funding, tools, and people to the project in the historic Joppa neighborhood. The Dallas-area Habitat for Humanity and a host of corporate sponsors and volunteers were also involved.

Around that time, we hosted a luncheon where we invited Cary out to speak to a small group of CEOs about why Hilti had moved to the area and what the community could do for them. At the conclusion of his presentation, I asked Cary, in front of about thirty CEOs, "What can we do to help you?" He stopped, then said he didn't know. I said, "Think about what you are passionate about. Where do you need a connection?"

He said, "Now that I think about it, we're painting some houses later this month and could use a hand." I asked for a show of hands. Now, mind you, these were CEOs. Yet the room proved full of volunteers. Some even offered to bring several employees out. Chris Durovich, CEO of Children's Health, ended up bringing more than thirty employees alone. Later that year, Hilti was awarded our YTexas Featured 50 award. Cary kicked off the event by coming onstage wearing a cowboy hat. Yes, a New Jersey guy in a cowboy hat. The crowd roared; Hilti had made their mark. That was the beginning of a great relationship with Hilti.

Shortly after first scratching the surface with Hilti, I got word that Cary was retiring. Hilti had announced that Avi Kahn, their Canadian market-organization general manager, was transferring to Dallas in November of 2016 to take over the role of president and CEO the following January. Avi, a native of Israel, had been with Hilti for twelve years, starting in an entry-level territory sales role before working through several positions that took him across the US and Canada. Prior to the move, Avi made periodic visits to Dallas from his residence in Canada.

Why Dallas?

Hilti has been seen on jobsites in the United States since the mid-1950s. At first, it was headquartered on the East Coast in Stamford, Connecticut. In 1979, the company relocated to Tulsa, Oklahoma, to find a more central location for a warehouse and headquarters. Even after the headquarters relocation, Hilti still maintains a very large operation center there, employing more than five hundred team members.

Hilti came to Dallas for a couple of reasons, including to be closer to a larger base of customers and to have access to a broader workforce as they continued to grow. The company hired a site-selection consultant about eighteen months prior to the move and had nineteen potential cities on their list, analyzing each location's quality of life, air service, operating costs, and labor market. During this time, the company visited with many chambers of commerce. In the end, it came down to choosing between Dallas and Chicago.

When asked what the decision boiled down to, Avi said a big factor was how Dallas showcased its benefits through organizations like the Dallas Regional Chamber and VisitDallas. In addition, Dallas had a great educational system and, with affordable housing, was positioned to allow employees to live in close proximity to the office. The strength of the local community and its closeness to some of Hilti's largest national customers were also main factors. Soon thereafter, the company moved its headquarters north of Dallas to Plano.

This reminds me of how Boeing decided to choose Chicago over Dallas for its world headquarters in the early '90s—an event that put Dallas in high gear, revitalizing the city and learning from the heartbreak. Ironically, as Avi and I spoke, he was staring out of his office window at Boeing Global Services, headquartered right next door.

Avi recalls visiting Dallas about once every month for his last position as general manager of Hilti in Canada. "One thing I recall is how everyone who relocated was so happy with their decision to move. It made me feel very comfortable moving myself."

The Execution

Once the decision was made to relocate the headquarters, the company communicated it very clearly, making timelines and resources available as soon as possible to allow employees time to digest the information and come to their own conclusions. "That's one of the things that really made me proud—how we supported our team members through this," said Avi. The company organized trips to the area for a few months so people and their families could see the region. About 75 percent of the people that were offered the opportunity to relocate did so. Hilti was very happy with that number considering the industry standard is well below that number.

The Dallas story is a strong one. It's about a four-hour drive from Tulsa, so people could still feel close to home. In addition, the company has a really strong culture, and most of the employees didn't want to walk away from that. "It was a fairly compelling story from the beginning," said Avi. The company retained many of its people, and most are still with the company today.

The Benefits of Texas

Avi has found so many personal benefits to living in Texas. It's been great for his family. His kids and his wife have a wonderful social circle, and the quality of the schools is nothing short of spectacular. "It's the most welcoming place I've ever lived," he said.

The state is also extremely business friendly, and when it comes to corporate giving, it's one of the strongest cultures Avi's seen. The positive feedback he heard from employees was that the housing and the postsecondary education system were great. The education system allowed them to see their kids enter the next phase of their lives by going to local universities. In addition, trailing spouses and partners did not have a problem finding work due to the strong job market. Lastly, both DFW and Love Field gave direct flights to anywhere in the world. For those who traveled, that was a big plus.

People's desire to make introductions and ask what they could do to help was unmatched. Dallasites value networking and take it seriously. On several occasions, he mentioned to people that he enjoyed public speaking; soon thereafter, his phone was ringing off the hook with speaking engagements on topics he was passionate about, such as the community and giving back. "There's always that desire to help each other and do the right thing."

Corporate Social Responsibility

Avi, a very involved corporate citizen, now chairs the international task force of the Dallas Regional Chamber. As the chair, he does admit that Dallas still runs into the old stigma about our cowboy roots. "We are working on that." Domestically, Dallas is in the game with pretty much every corporate relocation on the market. On the global level, however, there are still a lot of misconceptions about this region. On the top of the list is our influence in the tech industry. As part of this task force, Avi is helping raise this profile globally.

In typical fashion, Hilti continues to be very involved on the philanthropic side and encourages their team members to actively participate using their two paid community service days. They also have a focus on building their employer brand and attracting the right talent. One of Avi's priorities is to connect with talent and attract them to careers at Hilti. To that end, they provide training and education in the construction field, as well as very strong mentoring and development programs, earning them numerous employer awards.

Advice

"My advice is to come to Dallas–Fort Worth!" said Kahn. He said this is the future; this is where the opportunities are. "If I reflect on our process, I recall that we asked our consultants to help us with our most important issues. I suggest you ask yourself the same question: What is your most critical issue? Define these specific areas of focus."

In 2018, Hilti organized a visit for Michèle Frey-Hilti, the grand-daughter of company founder Martin Hilti, managing director of the Hilti Family Foundation Liechtenstein. She met with a number of non-profit organizations and community leaders here in DFW. As a global philanthropist, she was really impressed with the amount of work DFW has done to make life better here for women, particularly via vocational programs. She expected to see a prosperous region, but this came across particularly strongly to her. The trip brought to life the great work of Hilti and others in the area. "We have a commitment to give back to the communities where we live and work. That dimension of our corporate culture is consistent with all our markets around the world," said Avi. Dallas is no exception.

Chapter 11

Firefly Aerospace: Rocket Man

TOM MARKUSIC

It doesn't take a rocket scientist to figure out that Texas is friendly to business. Tom Markusic would agree, but he might argue that it's just as easy if you do happen to actually be a rocket scientist. Yes, Tom has the best answer to the casual line, "So tell me, what do you do?" He's a rocket scientist—and now a Texan. His entry into Texas came at the request of Elon Musk. In 2006, Elon asked whether he would be interested in running the SpaceX rocket test site in McGregor, Texas. Tom's answer was a resounding yes.

Tom's journey into the aerospace industry started with rather humble beginnings. He grew up in a very industrial, blue-collar town in northeastern Ohio. His dad was an autoworker who worked long days. Tom grew up working at a nearby Arabian horse farm. Tom's childhood was very secure and low pressure, instilling in him a sense of self-determination. He credits his success to the hands-off approach his parents had in his life, allowing him to be a curious student. Tom excelled in school and stayed local, attending Ohio State University. He was later accepted into Princeton as one of about ten PhD students worldwide to join the mechanical and aerospace engineering program. That secure life in northeastern Ohio was about to change. The journey was about to begin.

His first job out of Princeton was for the US Air Force, based at Edwards Air Force Base in California. From there, he headed to NASA in Huntsville, Alabama, working as a propulsion research scientist responsible for very futuristic projects. "Then, one day, they tapped me on the shoulder and said, 'Hey, we want you to go watch this crazy start-up company with this guy named Elon Musk who thinks he's going to do space different,'" said Tom. Next thing he knew, they'd sent him to Kwajalein Atoll, which is about an eight-hour flight from Hawaii on a small land mass in the middle of the Pacific called Omelek Island. Kwajalein has long been used by the United States for small research rocket launches due to its relative isolation in the South Pacific. The last US government rocket launch occurred in 1996.

After 2000, the island's location and nearby radar-tracking infrastructure attracted SpaceX, who updated the facilities on the island and established it as their primary launch location by 2006. SpaceX began launching Falcon 1 rockets from Omelek in 2006.

"When I arrived, I saw Elon and a few dozen people on a jungle island building a rocket and putting it together," said Tom. When he first met Elon, he was just reading management books and observing what they were doing. After a short period of time, he realized he was experiencing something amazing. The rocket launch did crash, but he was hooked. It was at that point that Elon offered him a job in Texas to run the SpaceX site. After five years with NASA, Tom decided to leave to join Elon and SpaceX in Texas.

SpaceX in McGregor, Texas

Tom enjoyed the South while working at NASA in Alabama. He was comfortable with the pace and the friendly nature of Southerners. When he got the call to move to Texas, his wife was six months pregnant with their fourth child. Needless to say, that transition was tough. Tom was excited to move to Texas and was not surprised at what he experienced when he arrived. The state's reputation of embracing independent thought was in line with what he'd experienced growing up as a kid, when people would leave him alone and allow him to creatively do his own thing. "Texas is what I thought then, and what I still think today, and why I'm still here now," said Tom. "It is one of the only places in the country where people don't get up in your business. The economic and regulatory climate is just amazing."

When Tom went to run the test site in McGregor, he paid a visit to the city manager. He had his plans in order to explain what they would be doing at the site and how they planned on complying with all the rules the city had for the facility. Tom was taken off guard at the reaction he got from the manager. "I remember his words exactly. He said, 'Son, just don't do anything I wouldn't do, OK?'" That really resonated with Tom and sticks with him today. The tongue-and-cheek comment sent the message that they expected him to do the right thing, make smart decisions, and be respectful of his neighbors. As long as he did that, he would be allowed to do his thing.

"Texas has an attitude that presumes innocence, not guilt, as you find in other states," said Tom.

Relocating Firefly to Texas

After five years of working for SpaceX, Tom moved on to a few other positions within the industry. He spent some time working for a couple other industry behemoths, including Jeff Bezos at Blue Origin in Seattle and Richard Branson at Virgin Galactic in California. In 2014, Tom founded Firefly Space Systems in Hawthorne, California. Soon thereafter, he planned his move back to Texas.

Firefly was essentially a start-up company. They purchased two hundred acres of land in a city called Briggs, Texas, to test their rockets while simultaneously relocating the corporate headquarters to Cedar Park, a northern suburb of Austin. When considering Cedar Park, Tom spoke to the city about his plans to lease space to employ high-paying engineers, software designers, and rocket scientists to design and build rockets that would launch small payload items into space. His mission was to bring an affordable US option to the market, which many other countries were looking to own.

When Tom met with Cedar Park officials, it was apparent that the city wanted him. He was overly impressed with how welcoming and helpful they were. "The local governments in Texas have resources to work with, and they are ready to spend them to help with economic development," said Tom. They city was laser focused on creating jobs to meet the demands of the surrounding areas, which were growing with residents. After little deliberation, Cedar Park was able to offer Firefly an incentive that would seal the deal. Since that time, despite the typical growing pains of a start-up company, Firefly has remained in Cedar Park and now employs more than two hundred people in the facility. In 2020, they plan to launch their first rocket into orbit.

The University of Texas also played a major role in their decision to move, as Cedar Park was in close proximity to the school. Firefly has employed students from the university to help with the design of their launch system.

When I asked Tom about moving people into the state, he told me something interesting: "Honestly, the most important reason we chose Austin was for the spouses." In the aerospace industry, families are often asked to relocate to remote places. The quality of life and education for the kids is not ideal. Tom mentioned his wife and kids often throughout our conversation. He and his wife have had four children in four different states and had moved their family seven times through the course of his career. It had been tough on the family. This time, he realized the decision had to work for everyone—not just for his family but for the families of his employees. When recruiting engineers, this is often challenging. Today, he competes with Bezos and Musk, so he knows he has to offer something a cut above the rest. Cedar Park fits the bill.

Texas offered them the perfect combination of a headquarters and manufacturing facility in a commercial and residential district with plenty of things to do for working and stay-at-home spouses. The school system was excellent as well. The Briggs facility is in relatively close proximity to the headquarters offices, which is a major plus. Options like this are hard to come by.

Advice from Tom

Tom was hesitant to give advice, as he compared giving advice on where to move a start-up company to giving someone marriage advice: it's a personal thing. There will be many challenges along the way no matter where you are.

What attracted Tom to Austin was its intersection of beliefs. Not everyone thinks the same way, which is healthy. Leverage everything that is different about the people and their various industries.

Tom noted that Texas is one of the few places in the country where you can live on a single income, as incomes are high enough and costs are low enough. The combination is unique.

As concerns start-ups, Tom would point out some myths that are not true. Austin, in his opinion, is not the next Silicon Valley. The type of investor here is a whole different animal, with a venture-capital community much more averse to risk than in California. You will likely not find the same level of risk tolerance in Texas as in other parts of the country.

If you're coming from a high-traffic city, you're going to find much of the same in Austin. He recommended moving to the fringes, where the gem of Austin is still easy to reach. Look at communities on the periphery.

Look into Opportunity Zones. They open up a whole new spigot of venture capital.

Don't be discouraged about moving to an area that doesn't have a foothold in your industry. Austin is not an aerospace city, and believe it or not, Firefly benefits from that. It is unique, and members of the company are treated like rock stars because they're different. Don't worry if your industry is not highly represented; it could be a competitive advantage.

Look to the future for your hiring needs. This year, Firefly Aerospace started Firefly Academy, a nonprofit STEM-promoting charity. The academy will provide hands-on expertise to students studying rocket science. Firefly Academy also pledged the University of Texas $1 million to train students to build rockets for future jobs in aerospace.

PART TWO

The Entrepreneur's Journey to Texas

Chapter 12

Texas Is Her Secret Weapon

KENDRA SCOTT

"You do good." Those were the inspiring words spoken to Kendra Scott by her stepfather, Rob, during the end of his fight with brain cancer. It was clear in my interview with Kendra that those words have lived with her every day since, from her early days as an entrepreneur to today, when she owns more than ninety retail jewelry stores across the country and has eclipsed $1 billion in valuation. I guess his inspiration helped. And yes, she did good.

Kendra Scott, for those of you who don't know, is a fashion icon who lives in Austin, Texas. Her journey to Texas started with a visit to her mother one summer. Kendra was finishing out high school in Kenosha, Wisconsin, with her father, but her mother lived in Houston with her stepfather, who worked for Compaq. "That summer, I absolutely fell in love with everything about Texas. I loved the people and the weather. It was like a tropical paradise compared to Wisconsin," Kendra laughed. She met a lot of kids her age that summer and couldn't believe how warm, friendly, and welcoming the people were. It was love at first sight—so she decided to move. "Houston was a new and exciting world for me," said Kendra of her first visit to the city. During her first winter in Houston, she recalls seeing her neighbor put up Christmas lights in a bathing suit. Coming from the Badger State, that was a first.

In her junior year, Kendra transferred from Wisconsin to Klein High School in Houston. She loved fashion and found that everyone at the school embraced her crazy ideas. It was very different than what she'd experienced in Wisconsin, where no one dreamed. At Klein, there were countless clubs and organizations that students could engage in. One that stood out to her was a group called Distributed Education Clubs of America (DECA). She picked apparels and accessories as her club profession and competed in that category. Two years in a row, she represented Klein at nationals.

It was clear that Kendra had a gift. Her aunt Joann (Aunt Jo) was a fashion director at Gimbels, and when Kendra was a child, Joann used to teach her how to trend forecast. She would project slide shows on her basement wall and give Kendra tours of her closet. Her aunt would let her dream by trying on her shoes, jewelry, and clothes in her gorgeous apartment on Wall Avenue in Milwaukee. "My aunt is an amazing woman," said Kendra. "She still is one of the most beautiful and glamorous women I know. Fashion, to me, was magic. It could transform you into anyone you wanted to be."

The Hat Box

When Kendra was nineteen years old, her stepfather, Rob, took a job in Austin with Dell Computers. Kendra, her mom, and Rob picked up and moved. Kendra intended to go to college, but life took over. Shortly after her move to Houston, Rob had been diagnosed with brain cancer. The move to Austin made it difficult for him to get to his cancer treatments at MD Anderson in Houston, arguably the best cancer treatment center in the world. Kendra and her mother were spending an incredible amount of time back in Houston at MD Anderson, but she felt it was important for her to spend this time with her mom. She was also building a great bond with Rob. So while others were having fun at school, she decided to skip school and help her mother. "I wouldn't change it for the world."

At MD Anderson, Kendra saw many women who were losing their hair and were searching for headwear. Kendra noticed that there weren't many comfortable options out there for women, especially those who were losing hair. Kendra had a collection of hats at home. She started sewing cotton linings into her hats and bringing them back to the hospital to give to patients. This is where her stepfather's inspiration took a foothold. He encouraged her to start a hat company. She knew her father had saved $25,000 for her to go to college, so she asked him whether she could use that college money to start a hat company. It didn't go over well at first. In the end, however, he approved, and the Hat Box was created.

The Hat Box was located in a good spot within the Highland Mall in Austin. Today, that mall, like most others, no longer exists. It has since been converted into Austin Community College. Kendra's business kept her on the road. She visited milliners all over Texas, including Stetson and others. Everyone was willing to show her the ropes. They even taught her how to mold hats. This is how Kendra first experienced the friendly business culture of Texas. She had a penchant for learning, and the hat business in Texas was fertile ground, particularly for women's options.

Kendra's heart always remained close to what had first encouraged her to start the venture: cancer patients. She set up private dressing rooms where women and men going through chemotherapy could try on an assortment of hats, including fun ones like fedoras and top hats. The business consumed her. She ran it seven days a week and was determined to have stores throughout the country.

The business had its ups and downs. There were times when things were tough, and she sometimes sold only a couple hats a day. She knew she wouldn't survive if things didn't change. Her mother helped when she could, sometimes wheeling her stepfather into the store. He had trouble speaking by that point, but he could understand everything and would beam with pride despite her situation. Then, on one visit, he asked her to come close. He couldn't speak loud enough for her to hear unless he spoke directly into her ear. He told her, "You do good." If you're finding this touching to read about, imagine what it was like to hear it from Kendra. I listened in tears. Kendra knew exactly what he meant, too. We have a short time on this earth; we should use the gifts we have been given to do something good.

A Lightbulb Moment

Kendra always loved jewelry, a passion going back to her days of exploring the fashion world with Aunt Jo. She loved vintage pieces. On her time off, which was infrequent, she went to beach shops and perused the stores. Jewelry was her way of relaxing—her escape from running a retail shop that was struggling.

She started stocking the Hat Box with jewelry that she'd made at home. It sold. She brought more, and she sold more. Toward the end of the Hat Box's life, she was selling virtually all of the jewelry she made immediately. It appeared her next venture was right in front of her.

After five years of running the Hat Box, she had to shut the doors. She was devastated. She had failed her dad and stepdad and was entering one of the lowest points of her life.

She had plenty of friends in Austin, so she reached out for work. A good friend, Matt O'Hare, gave her a job at Grand Adventures Tours. She moved up the ladder quickly and became director of advertising. In this job, she spent weeks touring destinations, in many cases for weddings. During her travels, she relaxed by sketching out designs of jewelry. She was always getting calls from past Hat Box customers asking about her jewelry, so she accommodated them by selling it on the side.

The travel was getting to Kendra, so she quit Grand Adventure, got married, and had a child. She was put on bed rest for part of her pregnancy and began tinkering with jewelry again, this time a lot. She took $500 out of the family's savings in order to put together her first collection of jewelry. She and her mother began taking the jewelry out in a wooden tea box and visiting local boutiques.

Again, she recalled how nice people were in learning about her jewelry. They offered her lemonade and bought sample sets from her.

"If I'd walked into a shop in New York or LA , they would have called security," Kendra said, laughing. Kendra went store to store, visiting every boutique in Austin that would take her. On her last stop, she closed a $1,200 order. The problem was that that was her entire inventory; Kendra gave the boutique owner every sample she'd made. She came home after that first day and told her husband, "We've got a business!"

Texas Support

I asked Kendra whether Texas had anything to do with her success. Her answer? "One million percent. A resounding yes." Her success at the boutiques in Austin absolutely made the Kendra Scott brand what it is today. The trunk shows in the community, the support of friends, and the house parties also helped tremendously. "It's a Southern thing. Texans are supportive of their own. They were proud of me and wanted me to succeed." She had a slew of loud and proud Texans with a network of megaphones.

Don't get me wrong; they truly loved the jewelry. One day, she got a call from someone in Dallas. "Hello, are you Kendra?" the caller asked.

"Yes, I am."

"Who *are* you? None of my stores are carrying any other lines, and yours are falling off the shelf! Can you come to Dallas?"

Kendra immediately hit I-35 and headed for Dallas. When they spoke in person, it was clear to her that the buyer wanted to carry her line, and in mass quantities. Keep in mind that Kendra was still producing the jewelry out of her bedroom, covering her dining-room table with orders. The buyer placed an order for $75,000. Kendra cried. "Jennifer," she said, "you just made someone the happiest person in the world." This buyer happened to be Harold's, a Dallas-based chain of high-end ladies' and men's specialty apparel in traditional, classic styles. It was where all of the who's who went.

Jennifer told Kendra that she'd never had anyone cry about an order. She was used to dealing with large companies out of big cities that expected the business. In reality, I don't think Jennifer realized how early of a stage Kendra Scott was at. It didn't matter. The jewelry did all the talking.

"At this point, we had a real business," said Kendra. She began production overseas and started producing several thousand pieces. Kendra had met her market: Texas. She loved the story, and the story loved her. An iconic Texas brand had given her a chance, and she was about to return the favor—and do good.

Why Texas?

Kendra feels it's important to know that Texas is an amazing place for business, for companies of any size. Often, when she told buyers she was from Austin, Texas, they would say, "Texas?" and smirk. "Isn't Texas just Western?"

"No, it's not, actually," Kendra would say back. This attitude frustrated her, but she remained polite. "They would always tell me that you could not build a real fashion brand out of Texas. If it weren't on the coast, it wouldn't have a chance." This lit a fire under Kendra, as she loves it when someone tells her she can't do something. "I knew these people had never been here. I knew they didn't know our culture, vibrancy, and creativity."

It was at that point Kendra knew she could win. Kendra Scott, the brand, had her own unique interpretation of what people wanted: how to mix color and stand out. Customers loved what they were designing and couldn't care less where they were from. Sure enough, Kendra began killing the competition. "Without a doubt, our brand is Texas. Being in Austin definitely gives us a competitive edge. Honestly, it's our secret weapon."

Kendra learned a lot about the industry on the coasts, but honestly, she wanted to do things differently. She'd seen the rundown offices in New York where people worked till the crack of dawn, but she applied a work-life balance to her personal situation, as she wanted to be a more present mother. Kendra Scott is revolutionizing the fashion industry by giving balance and meaning that support women and their families. She wants the company to be something bigger. She is indeed living up to Rob's reminder to do good.

Now, Kendra has built a world-renowned fashion brand that is mentoring designers in Texas. She's excited to see more consumer packaged goods companies moving into the area. She sees a bright future in Texas of embracing funding sources and incubators for small- and medium-sized business. Kendra is quite optimistic about business prospects in Texas. "I really think the top is going to be blown off of what is going on. With more and more businesses moving here, I think we're going to see a bigger Texas takeover across the country." It's a dynamic place that has all the good things about New York and Los Angeles but leaves the worst things behind.

I asked Kendra what her plans are for the future. "I feel like we've just now scratched the surface after seventeen years," she said, laughing. The company is growing internationally and aims to be the best in jewelry. "Never be complacent, and always be innovating and exciting." One such innovation is the future of augmented reality and virtual reality in the industry. Kendra is already testing out products—including some that were featured at South by Southwest—that allow you to try on hundreds of pieces of jewelry virtually. They certainly want to be part of this trend.

Before our interview concluded, Kendra told another interesting story about her experiences in Texas. It occurred during one of her most trying times. The recession had hit, and businesses were shuttering. At the time, Kendra Scott was only a wholesaler, with no retail stores of her own. She knew she had to establish a direct connection to her customers, or her livelihood would be in the hands of her distributors. Her largest customer, Harold's, had just filed for bankruptcy.

One day, she got a call from her bank. They were closing down her line of credit due to her high-risk industry. She knew that if this happened, she would be closed down. She had never been late on a payment and was making money. She pleaded with the banker, but to no avail.

She was referred to a woman named Kerry Hall at Texas Capital Bank. "I walked into her office and said, 'I promise you, I will pay you every penny back. I'll give you every asset I have. I need your help.'" Texas Capital delivered—and remains her bank to this day. Kendra now sits on their board. I mentioned Texas Capital in my opening chapter about my first years in Texas. What a coincidence!

Kendra Scott's Core Values: Family, Fashion, and Philanthropy

If there is a company in Texas that understands the meaning of philanthropy, it's Kendra Scott.

Kendra has taken living up to Rob's reminder to do good to another level. This year, the company invested $250,000 in a grant for metastatic breast cancer research with the Breast Cancer Research Foundation, supporting an amazing female doctor at Baylor College of Medicine who is leading the charge in this field.

Kendra is also giving back to MD Anderson, the hospital that gave her the gift of time with her stepfather. It welcomed the Kendra Cares program with open arms. Through this program, Kendra Scott brings their Color Bar to patients so they can pick out stones and frames to create jewelry that will bring joy to their day. Today, more than thirty hospitals around the state participate in the program.

Kendra Scott also works a lot with Andy Roddick and his wife, Brooklyn Decker. "Andy and Brooke are dear, dear, dear friends of ours," said Kendra. "We enjoy supporting the Andy Roddick Foundation." She also works with Camila and Matthew McConaughey's foundation, Just Keep Livin.

Advice from Kendra

Kendra believes it's important to realize that in Texas, people give and care about their community. It goes far beyond philanthropy. People in Texas care so much about community. "When I lost Rob at such a young age, I took his three words to heart. I wanted to create a company that would give back. I wanted to do good. I had a passion for fashion. Now I have a supportive family, and I want to be present as a mom. You can do the same. In New York, people want to revolutionize the industry, but they are often run down and overworked. Here, we have balance. If you're in the fashion industry, consider Texas. You don't need to be on the coasts."

In Texas, other fashion brands, designers, and entrepreneurs will answer the phone. Even when her brand was small, Kendra could pick up the phone, call fifty entrepreneurs, and ask for advice. People help each other. Kendra would urge readers to pick up the phone; people will answer. "Our competition is the world. Here, Texans want to win and help each other. Join forces and hands. It's very different from other places. We use our knowledge and invest in one another. I'm excited to be a part of this community and excited to see it flourish."

The attitude in Austin is that anything is possible. There is a diverse community of musicians, politicians, and business people. Throw in the University of Texas, and you have an amazing culture. You'll see bankers having coffee with musicians. Everyone is inspired by each other. For Kendra, that undoubtedly helped. She has more than ninety stores and a valuation of more than $1 billion despite having no college or formal fashion training. Be inspired by Austin's diversity.

Chapter 13

The Four-Hour Texan

TIM FERRISS

Imagine writing a book for a few friends, submitting it to—oh, I don't know—maybe twenty-seven publishers, and finding out soon thereafter that you are world famous. That's what happened to Tim Ferriss after the first twenty-six publishers said his book didn't have a chance. With the help of the twenty-seventh and only about ten thousand copies of *The 4-Hour Workweek*, he became a phenomenon. However, he was no one-hit wonder. In fact, he's managed to transform his unplanned fame and intriguing mind into a brand recognized around the world. Today, his podcast, *The Tim Ferriss Show*, in which he interviews some of the best minds in the world, has garnered more than four hundred million downloads. And now, it's right here in Austin, Texas.

I'm a huge fan of Tim. I've read *The 4-Hour Workweek*, oh, about one hundred times. It's one of those timeless books. In 2017, more than ten years after it was written, it was the most-highlighted book on Amazon, and it is still the most-quoted book on Amazon today. As of now, it has sold more than three million copies and counting.

In 2006, I was moving up the corporate ladder in my banking career and had accumulated a dozen or so rent houses in my spare time, which was not very spare. I was enamored with the fact that passive income could generate almost as much cash flow as a full-time corporate job where I had to sport a tie, slap on the cologne, and format PowerPoints. The real-estate business was a blast, but the only thing passive about it was the income. Both my gigs were labor intensive. Tim's book hit home with me and got my creative juices going. Today, my wife and I use many of his tactics in our businesses. Interestingly, one of the two friends he wrote the book for was a banker.

In 2009, he wrote *The 4-Hour Body*. Soon after I started reading it, I wondered whether I needed to go to med school just to understand it. I loved it because it was entertaining—and, again, thought provoking. The book was the result of his three-year quest to find the smallest change in human behavior that would effect the biggest results in terms of weight loss and fitness. He did outrageous things for the book, like extracting muscle tissue from his leg to determine how much fast-twitch muscle fiber he had. In short, he was A/B testing his body like you would a start-up. To give you the short version of his findings: Ingest thirty grams of protein within thirty minutes of waking, have a nap and casual sex in the afternoon, and eat two tablespoons of almond butter before you go to bed. Throw in two thirty-minute workouts per week (for a total of four hours a month), and you'll be svelte. Tim proved his point by gaining thirty-four pounds of muscle in twenty-eight days while losing three pounds of fat. The concept of smart work and fitness for maximum results sold.

Four years ago, Tim decided to start a podcast. At the time, many of his friends and colleagues told him he was too late; the podcast ship had sailed. Like he was going to listen, anyway. Today, Tim's podcast has a larger reach than all of his books combined, with over four hundred million downloads and a few million unique visitors to the website. He interviews people from all walks of life, dissecting patterns in the behavior of world-class performers, CEOs, and entrepreneurs.

There's No Bubble in Texas

In 2018, Tim moved from Silicon Valley to Austin. It's been a long road, but he's never been happier. He first wanted to move to Austin right after college in 1999–2000, but his final interview with Trilogy didn't pan out. He landed a job in Silicon Valley instead. A visit to South by Southwest in 2007 reignited his desire to live in the Lone Star State, and during each SXSW visit since (nearly every year), he spent more and more time exploring the area.

Beginning in 2015 or so, Tim began to feel that the coastal areas were turning into bubbles of like-minded thinking where collaboration and creativity were no longer colliding. Silicon Valley's culture—a mind-set of always trying to be at the forefront of ideas, coupled with a fear of missing out—was something he couldn't handle any more.

His experiences in Austin have been quite the opposite. "The Texas entrepreneur is different." He found not only that people were more open and less smug but that the diversity of industries and professions aided his podcast and his life interests more. "I could be having breakfast with the CEO of a midmarket business, then lunch with an oil and gas investor, then dinner with a film producer." People in these industries are underrepresented in places like Silicon Valley or the Bay Area. For the most part, cities like New York are centered around financial discussion, and DC is all politics. Texas has everything.

That diversity is what makes Austin, and Texas in general, a hotbed for healthy collaboration. "It's how business should be done."

While Tim is not outwardly political, he has also found the mix of conservative and progressive thinking much more healthy than in other parts of the US. "It is a true republic." While each region of the state does possess a different culture—with, say, Houston and Austin having different vibes—Tim has found that their values are similar and that most people are on the same page regarding where they want things to go. He enjoys that the political mix here is much less hostile.

Texas Pride

Tim has spent only about one year in Texas, so many of his experiences continue to be firsts.

Like many of the people I've interviewed, he loves Texas's pride. He's found that when he meets someone from West Texas at an airport overseas and asks them where they are from, they say West Texas—not the US. He finds that intriguing. Most people refer to their state at most. In Texas, they give you the exact part of the state.

Also, even if you've met one Texan, you haven't met them all. It's a gigantic state with a lot of rich culture. The vastness of the Lone Star State is something Tim is eager to explore. He wants to journey out to areas like Marfa, where there is a lot going on. He also admires the fact that no one leaves Texas. He's met many people who could possibly achieve more in their business, even fame or fortune, if they moved to, say, New York or LA. Yet so many people make it work here, even if their chances for success might be higher in other states.

Tim's entire podcast consists of studying people who live outside of the mainstream and like to do things differently than the rest. The fact that Texans are, in some ways, uncompromising is what will make Tim's podcast a big success in Texas. I feel he can make us a success in return.

Chapter 14

A Three-Year Plan Turned Twenty

Harry LaRosiliere, mayor of Plano, Texas

The mayor of Plano, Harry LaRosiliere, is a very popular guy in the DFW metroplex. He always has a smile on his face, and when I first met him for our interview, my best time with him was off camera. We talked about New York and how our transitions had gone. Coincidentally, he'd gone to Cardinal Hayes, a Catholic high school in the Bronx not far from where my father went several years earlier. Mayor LaRosiliere is gaining fame primarily from his astounding record in drawing corporate relocations to his city from all over the world. He's had CEOs beg him to run for reelection and was instrumental in luring Toyota to his city. He asked the representatives from Toyota what the company wanted in a city, and they told him they wanted a place where their people would want to live. Harry said, "Congratulations—you've found your home." I always thought that was a great closing statement. It's no wonder Plano is a darling city to companies looking at Texas.

From Harlem to Plano

Prior to moving to Texas, Harry spent his entire life in New York City. In fact, he was in New York during our interview, visiting with his mother in the apartment he'd grown up in. Harry grew up in Harlem, in the shadows of the Cotton Club and a mile from the Apollo Theater, right in the thick of things. He was born in Haiti, and his parents immigrated to New York when he was about three years old.

Harry came to Texas on January 1, 1994. He came with his then girlfriend, now wife, who came to work for Frito-Lay right out of grad school. Their plan was temporary and similar to many, including mine. They intended to hang out and get their careers started, then head back to New York—"because," as he put it, "there was no way we would stay in Texas." As Harry joked, when you leave New York, New Yorkers say you are going nowhere.

He had a three-year plan. As of today, he's about twenty-one years into it.

Harry's wife started working for Frito-Lay in marketing. He had studied geology in New York and had started a photography studio out of college, but he'd just sold his photography business, bought out by a larger company in 1993. He intended to go back to school to become a psychologist. In the meantime, he found a position as a financial advisor, and he's been doing that ever since. His advisory job grew, and today, he is on UBS's top team in the Southwest region and one of the top in the nation.

When he sold his business, he read the book *What Color Is Your Parachute?* It took him through a decision tree and a battery of questions. The conclusion he reached was that he wanted to help people and to have an income based on ability that had time flexibility but was in a professional environment. He didn't see financial advisor on the list of possible careers; he did see psychologist. So he figured he would make some money and go to school at night to become a psychologist, using his position in financial advising as a placeholder until he graduated. "It's a tough industry," said the mayor. "You eat what you kill—and if you're good, you can make a lot of money. If not, you make no money. It fit the bill, and I haven't looked back since."

Why Mayor?

After arriving in Texas, he became very active in the community, getting involved in nonprofits and spending six years on the Plano City Council. In 2013, he became the first African American mayor of Plano.

He's a wealth manager with UBS and essentially has two full-time jobs. One, he says, pays him real income; the other, spiritual. He is on his second term as mayor, having been first elected in 2013 and then reelected in 2017. His second term will end in 2021. More and more frequently, people ask him whether his political career will continue past being mayor. "People think I'm being coy about it, but I've never envisioned myself going past mayor."

He first decided he wanted to become a mayor in 1993; he just didn't know it was going to be in Plano. At the time, he planned on being mayor of New York. His interest in the position was sparked by an incident in an area of Brooklyn called Crown Heights. This area was home primarily to West Indians and Hasidic Jews, all socioeconomically challenged. It was an odd mix.

During a funeral precession, a man lost control of his car, and a West Indian boy was killed. The Jewish EMS came (Hasidic Jews had their own ambulances) and attended to the man in the car before attending to the boy. This incident aggravated something that had already been bubbling up. The next day, a Jewish man got pulled out of his car and beaten. Harry perceived that David Dinkins—the mayor at the time and the city's first African American mayor—was being passive about the matter, hesitating to come down on the community and neglecting to send enough police in to calm things down. "I was disappointed because the mayor's role is to be the soul of the city. It was his chance to be great. That's what I felt," said Harry. "That was my calling. I said, 'I'm going to be mayor someday.'"

I asked the mayor how he'd felt about coming to the South. By the time he moved to Plano, he wasn't a *young* black man—but he fit the profile if someone chose to profile him. "A concern was always there, but not more so because I was in Texas." He remembers that when he was growing up, his father rooted against the Dallas Cowboys because Dallas was where JFK had been killed. "It was odd, but that was the mind-set I had. My first experience of Texas was in Plano. It was much less developed at the time, but Dallas certainly had the metro feel."

Settling in Texas

Harry described his drive to Texas as *Beverly Hillbillies* in reverse. He packed up, left New York, and drove eight hours directly to North Carolina. From there, he drove another eighteen hours straight. He wouldn't stop anywhere there wasn't a major league baseball team. "There was no way I was stopping in Louisiana at 11:00 p.m. at night," Harry laughed. "I was drinking coffee the whole night." He certainly had some preconceptions.

When he arrived in Texas, it was the first time in his life he felt like a true minority. The Catholic grammar school he'd attended in the South Bronx was predominantly black and Hispanic. He'd grown up in Harlem, and New York was a very diverse and multicultural city. At the time, Plano was about 4 or 5 percent African American. Today, it's 8 percent. In his office, he was one of two African American employees out of seventy-five total.

"In general, I was accepted," said Harry. What he found when he worked in financial advising was that it was easy to go out into the community and gain credibility. He first joined the chamber of commerce. Then, he was asked to serve on a committee or two. Shortly thereafter, he was invited to join Rotary International—an invitation-only group.

People started to notice him. This led to local boards and then to a commission for the city, which led to the council. "The spirit of acceptance is what opened the path for me that led me to where I am today," said Harry. "In New York, I would have had to fight for it. It wouldn't have happened organically."

Texas has been very welcoming to Harry. He never felt like he didn't belong. No one outwardly treated him differently, and that was a pleasant surprise to him. "When you are a majority minority, it is different."

Harry's wife retired fourteen years ago. The trigger point was the birth of their daughter in 1997. By then, they had settled into the fact that they were staying. He hadn't realized how difficult New York had been until he was gone. It was a grind and a fight, a struggle every day. Growing up, that was all he'd known. In Texas, the pace was easier. He didn't have to elbow his way through lines or onto the subway. In Texas, at first it felt odd when people smiled as they greeted him. Waiters in New York feel like they are doing a favor for you. In New York, if you make eye contact with someone, that's an aggressive move. In Texas, it's just the start of a conversation. In New York, you hold on to your pockets and try to predict the next move. "When I go back to New York, I flip the switch. I don't smile as much."

Why Plano?

In Plano, Harry got involved by volunteering for many nonprofits, in particular Court Appointed Special Advocates (CASA), a nonprofit for abused children. He sat on that board and was also on a committee for the Boys & Girls Clubs, as well as being involved with the Rotary club and Leadership Plano. At the time, Plano had only about 250,000 residents, which seemed small to a New Yorker. These nonprofit roles and his reputation in the market led him to being pointed to countless boards for the City of Plano.

In 2005, he was elected to the city council. The mayor at the time had suggested he run for council, and he beat a thirty-five year veteran in an upset. He served two three-year terms, then took a few years off. Then, when the standing mayor decided not to run for reelection, Harry threw his hat into the ring. In 2013, he ran for mayor of Plano and won.

Plano has great schools, and the cost of living is much less than in many parts of the US. Plano is also a safe city, with better ease of mobility. "Texans are spoiled. In New York, I had a ninety-minute commute. Here, people complain about a twenty-five minute commute."

I could relate to Harry's morning routine in New York. In a two-year period, in New York, Harry's car was stolen once and broken into three times. He had an alarm and a lock, and every morning, after he got up from the alarm, he went through a three-point checklist. First, he would check to see whether the car were there. Then, when he got to the car, he would check whether the battery were there. Last, he would check to see whether he still had a radio. If all three checks passed, he started the day. Every day began like this, and then it was off to his ninety-minute commute.

Now he lives in Plano, of course, annually cited as one of the safest cities in America. In twenty-four years in Plano, his car has been broken into once, when he inadvertently left it unlocked. The intruder rummaged through the glove compartment but didn't take anything. "I would never have left it unlocked in New York."

Advice from Mayor LaRosiliere

"There are plenty of doors here to go through," said Harry. "Education opens doors; what you do in the room is up to you." Texas has an abundance of opportunities if you're willing to put your hard hat on and work. Harry feels that the grind-it-out mentality of New York helped him. Every time he goes back, he realizes how soft he's become. "I used to be pretty intense, but now I'm about 50 percent of what I was in New York.

"I think you will find life challenging if you don't get connected here," he added. "If you're African American, you have to go out and find your peers." He had to actively seek out organizations where his kids could find others that looked like them. There is a lot more diversity in Dallas than in Plano or Frisco, but that is changing. With the influx of global corporations, there is now more diversity in Collin County that will allow you to find those connections. That was not the case twenty years ago.

Harry's advice is to be open to exploring. It's easy to have a stereotype about a place in mind and then reinforce it with your behavior. If you think Texans are a bunch of rednecks who won't accept you, you'll reinforce that preconception with what you perceive. Be open to seeing the richness of Texas's diversity. Plano is almost 45 percent non-Caucasian, with 18 percent of the population being Asian, 17 percent Latino, and 8 percent African American. Plano schools are more than 60 percent non-Caucasian. Be willing to explore and expand your mind-set and boundaries.

If you're moving here for a career, work hard. Anywhere you go in the US and in life, you will rise to the level that you choose. "I'd like to say I would still be where I am if I were anywhere, but it's easier in Texas," said Harry. There are fewer impediments in Texas because the quality of life, pace, and resources are not like in New York.

If Harry could do anything differently, he would have come to Texas sooner. Being a New Yorker means living in a bubble. It's them against the world—kind of a bunker mentality—and no one else understands them. At the time, Harry couldn't see a world past that. Also, he would have been more aggressive in encouraging family to move here. He never thought about recruiting family, but he does visit New York as often as he can.

Harry was a prototypical New Yorker, and being mayor of Plano was hard for him to fathom at first. Now, he's accepted the idea and settled in. Quite honestly, by now, he once thought he'd be back home in New York. His wife jokes, "Here you were wanting to go back home to New York, and now you are Mr. Plano." But he wouldn't leave to go anywhere else!

Around the year 2000, about six years after Harry moved here, he was in his former workplace, and he thought, *You know, when I first moved here, I thought it would be all big hats, big boots, and big hair. But actually, it's pretty normal here.* Then, over the office intercom, he heard, "Billy Bob on hold for Jimmy Jack." He got a chuckle out of that.

Chapter 15

In with a White Coat, and Out with a White Horse

OLIVIER CHAVY,
FORMER CEO OF WILSON & ASSOCIATES

Olivier Chavy is larger than life. He's tall, dark, and handsome, and to top it off, throw on a French accent. No, I'm not jealous. Who really wants to be tall, dark, and handsome with a funny accent? What's larger than his appearance is his heart—and his resume.

I was introduced to Olivier through a mutual friend, Mina Chang. Mina was the CEO of Linking the World, a humanitarian aid organization, who relocated her headquarters to Dallas from South Korea. She, too, was larger than life—and still is. She now resides in Washington, DC. Even though Olivier and Mina have now left Texas, they both left a lasting impression on the state. As you will see in this chapter, it left a lasting impression on Olivier as well.

A Life-Changing Event

Born and raised in France, Olivier first visited Texas in 1987. Then a twenty-year-old MBA student at Cornell University, he did a six-month internship in Texas for a company based out of Dallas. At the conclusion of this internship, the owner of the company gave him a gift: a white horse. Yes, a real white horse!

Olivier was in shock. He didn't know what to say. "I told him, 'One day, I will come back to Dallas, Texas,'" said Olivier. It was an adventure, a dream come true after having come from France. The internship opportunity in Dallas was one of his best souvenirs of America. The horse, unfortunately, had to stay.

After he graduated from Cornell, Olivier worked all over the world, including in France, Washington, DC, and Florida. After twelve years running hotels with a French group, he was the youngest general manager of Palace in Europe. In 2000, he joined Hilton for twelve years, holding such positions as general manager, senior vice president of operations, and global head of luxury brands performances. He traveled 260 days a year to 106 countries, so I guess you'd say he's seen a few places.

A Return to Texas

Then, in 2015, his dream was fulfilled: he was to return to Dallas, this time as the CEO of an established, Dallas-based global interior design firm, Wilson & Associates. Most of the hotels in Dallas, including the Anatole and the Mansion, were designed by Wilson. They have a huge legacy in Texas. It must have been fate, because when Olivier came to Wilson for his first day of work, he noticed that the firm was located on a well-known street in Dallas called Turtle Creek. Before relocating to Dallas, Olivier's home street had also been called none other than—you guessed it—Turtle Creek!

The transition to CEO of Wilson was very good for Olivier. He had been hired by the private-equity firm that owned Wilson, which required him to interview with the entire leadership team, so Wilson chose him rather than him choosing them. Luckily for him, the leadership and the culture of the company were there before he stepped in. He worked on projects all over the world with Wilson but found that the culture was the same in every office. This made his job easy.

By far what most made Olivier want to come back to Dallas was how nice people were. Some of the people at the ranch he'd stayed at had never left it, and many had never left Texas. They had no clue where France was, but that was what made them so authentic, so nice, and so welcoming. Olivier felt like part of the family. They took such good care of him that he wanted to live there again one day. Compared to Cannes, France, Texas was like a different planet—yet he still wanted to come back one day.

The Benefits of Being in Texas

Interior design has a big market share in Texas. According to Olivier, the pool of talent here is one clear benefit. Dallas, Austin, and Houston all have national architectural firms. If you look at the skylines in these major metros, you can see that the state has an affinity for architecture. Because of the easy lifestyle in Texas, many in the industry want to move here.

Frequent travel is common for professionals in this industry, so the DFW airport was critical to Olivier. "I was commuting twice a month to Shanghai, China. Getting in and out from Dallas was amazingly easy, and I have to say, the infrastructure in Dallas is second to none." He often took the train to the airport. For local flights, Love Field and Southwest Airlines were other major advantages of the area. Shortly after he arrived, he transferred the corporate travel accounts to Southwest after spending a luncheon listening to Gary Kelly, the CEO of Southwest.

The third benefit was the networking. Within six months, he felt like more than a citizen; he felt like part of a family. He was able to start an amazing network that brought him so much personally and professionally. His networking was so powerful that he came close to merging the firm with a large Texas-based architectural firm.

Olivier doesn't think the size of your company makes a difference. As a vendor in Texas, he was exposed to huge companies as well as to start-ups. Everyone, from the chamber of commerce to the tourism board, was all in it together. "Overall, my experience in Texas was unbelievable."

A clear challenge for Olivier was the Texas weather. In managing Wilson, he saw a slowing of activity in June, July, and August because of the heat. At first, he thought that could potentially affect productivity. Luckily, since Wilson was a global company, a slowdown in Texas would not have a major effect on the business as a whole. If his business had been local, though, it could have affected them. "It's more than one hundred degrees in the summer, and a lot of people leave to get away from the heat. I felt that the city and the state slowed down during the summer."

A Texas Health-Care Experience

"I'm the only Frenchman who doesn't drink alcohol or coffee or smoke," said Olivier. "I live a very healthy life. I don't even gamble." Olivier had a health issue while he was in Dallas and required heart surgery for something called an ablation. Everything worked out fine, but Olivier didn't say anything about it to his family. "I have to tell you, the health system was amazing." The hospitals in Dallas were amazingly efficient; he recalls doing a check-up by video one day with a doctor based in Houston. He even was able to check his blood pressure remotely. Olivier asked his personal doctor in France what they would've done, and they told him the Texas doctors had done an amazing job. "I was very secure about health care in Texas."

Texas Hospitality

Olivier began to tell me a story that I had heard, but never in so much detail. I had introduced Olivier to Donnie Nelson, president of basketball operations for the Dallas Mavericks. Donnie is a magnanimous man in town. One day, Olivier told Donnie that his son, who was seventeen years old, needed to do a one-week internship and wanted to major in sports management. Olivier asked Donnie whether he could do something, and Donnie said sure, send him over. When Olivier brought his son to the American Airlines Center, Donnie opened up the door wearing his boots and his hat. He's very Texan. "He took my child, opened up the warehouse with the sneakers and jerseys and sports gear and so on, and said, 'Help yourself, and get ready,'" said Olivier. I couldn't believe that when I heard it.

Donnie then took him to the practice court. He stopped the training and told the guys, "This is the new CEO of the company. He'll be with us for a week, so I want you to play ball with him for the next couple of hours. Then he'll come to my office to work with me." It didn't stop there. Donnie spent the next four days with Olivier's son. He asked him for help with some trade feedback. He went over all the statistics of the players. He even involved him in a trade meeting. His son still talks about it to this day.

When Olivier told me this story, he exclaimed, "This was Donnie Nelson of the Dallas Mavericks. Unbelievable! He treated my son like his own. This internship was not mopping the floors; he was the CEO of the Mavericks." Donnie actually stopped Dirk Nowitzki while he was playing and said, "Hey, play with this guy."

"Only in Texas," said Olivier. Donnie made Olivier feel like a friend for life. They often speak candidly about personal and business issues, and Olivier considers Donnie a special friend. On a separate occasion, Olivier flew to Paris with Donnie and introduced him to the CEO and chairman of the Paris Saint-Germain (PSG) team. Their relationship is solid.

Advice from Olivier

Olivier has some advice for any French people relocating to Texas. "Don't try to change your behavior or the way people are living or eating. Just adapt yourself. They have great traditions here, so just adapt your ways to the Texas lifestyle."

I asked Olivier how he felt in Texas, as an international transplant. Olivier said, "The people in Texas showed me total respect. It's very difficult in America when you're coming from France to make friends. Here, we go to dinner at each other's houses like we do in France, but here you have a much bigger network because people care. The entrepreneurial spirit in Texas is key to keeping the network alive."

What Olivier felt in Texas, he did not feel in other states. He found that many offices here have a philanthropic mind-set of giving back. He learned of a chef in town who would only hire juveniles. Linking the World, Mina Chang, and so many others stood out to him. "This was a surprise to me. I think giving back is part of the DNA in Texas."

If you're moving to Texas, try not to do it by yourself. The network is there; just open the door, and people will be more than happy to help. People are willing to welcome you and help at every level, whether in school, family, health, work, or business.

Olivier's time back in Dallas came to a halt when he successfully transacted the very first acquisition of an American company by a Chinese state-owned company via a free trade zone. This was a big deal in China and a windfall for Wilson. Fortunately, the firm left Wilson's headquarters in Dallas.

Once the Chinese firm bought Wilson, they took it public on the Shanghai stock exchange. For financial and tax reasons, Olivier could not stay any longer. He moved on in his career and became CEO of Mövenpick Hotels & Resorts for three years. Mövenpick sold to the

Accor Group, and after one year, Olivier announced a new position in America. "I'm looking forward to settling in America. My kids are in Florida and Washington, DC. My youngest son is at the University of Arizona." Olivier is now the president and CEO of RCI, a listed global company leader in the timeshare exchange with forty-two hundred properties affiliated and more than four million members.

Chapter 16

A Ride with Jack LaLanne

Larry North, CEO of Larry North Fitness

If you are an entrepreneur interested in moving to Texas, Larry North's path to stardom could provide some sage advice. You will hear over and over that Texas is a difficult place in which to raise capital. That's true for venture-capital money for a technology start-up, maybe. But for a low-tech business concept that doesn't require several rounds of fundraising, it's not. Larry was able to build an empire by building relationships. His strategy was to hang out with the rich and famous. What did that get him? His own wealth and fame.

Before this interview, I had never met or spoken to Larry North. Several months prior, I'd connected with him on LinkedIn. I had no particular reason to connect other than the fact that he and I had a lot of mutual friends. At the time, I wasn't even planning to write this book.

Larry North is a fitness legend in Texas. But the story of his move to Texas and rise to fame is more legendary than his name. Larry credits a drive with Jack LaLanne to his hard work and motivation. Jack's advice to Larry: do it on your terms, and be your own legend. Larry never forgot that.

Larry has written three books, including the best-selling *Living Lean*, and created one of the top-selling weight-loss shows in the country, *The Great North American Slim Down*. It grossed more than $120 million in sales and was ordered by more than one million people. Larry also hosts a show on KRLD radio that has been running for several years.

Larry is only seven years older than I am, but I've always thought of him as a staple in Dallas, even when I first moved there in 1993. My first apartment in Dallas was in the Village, a place where most youngsters in Dallas flopped. Larry lived there, too, at one point. I bartended at a prominent restaurant called the 8.0, where we had a menu item called the "North Plate"—Larry's signature meal. From what I remember, it was chicken and broccoli or something like that.

I worked out at his gym a couple of times, but only as a guest. His first club was in Highland Park Village, a swanky neighborhood where a kid from the Village would only aspire to hang out.

Interviewing Larry for this book was a pleasure and, I have to say, one of my favorite interviews. Larry moved here in 1978, long before I did, but not under the best of circumstances. He was fifteen years old, a Brooklyn native with a strong New York accent, and the father figure in his family.

His Break from New York

Our interview started with an intense conversation about Larry's father, who was the reason he left New York. His path to Texas was not intentional; it was really just something he stumbled upon. Larry's father, whom he referred to as Irv, was profiled on *60 Minutes* twice, in 1976 and in 1986. Irv was a degenerate compulsive gambler and New York mobster. He had a rough life and was abusive to Larry's mother, who tried countless times to get away from him. A successful break came when Larry was fifteen years old. Larry, his mom, and his twin younger brothers made a desperate attempt to get out of New York, heading to Las Vegas in a beat-up old car. They chose Vegas primarily because Irv was banned from Vegas at that time, so they knew he wouldn't show up there. Fleeing didn't go without a hitch; they made it only to New

Jersey before the car broke down. "We finally got to Vegas at the beginning of the summer, but my mom just couldn't do it. She said, 'I can't raise my kids in their father's temple.'" However, she would not go back to anyplace where Irv could trace them, such as Los Angeles or New York. Nobody knew where they were. Larry's mother randomly picked Houston, Texas, because there was no legal gambling in the state. She wanted to start a fresh life.

So, from Vegas, they headed to Houston. One of the main expressways to Houston was I-75 (Central Expressway). Their route followed I-75 to I-45, then I-45 all the way to Houston. This time, they got pretty far before their car broke down for the final time. Larry remembers it vividly. "We broke down at the Spring Valley exit in a city called Richardson, Texas." With minimal funds, they stayed in a roach motel for five weeks until their mother was able to get on her feet. It was a rough go for the North family.

Larry told me that if it weren't for Jewish Family Services and the Baptist community in Dallas, they might not have made it. His twin brothers were only five at the time. The family had a pact that they wouldn't tell a soul where they were. Larry ultimately broke that pact when he called a friend to let him know they were safe. "I called from a pay phone and said, 'Listen, we're safe in Texas, that's all I can tell you.' My friend said, "You know, our neighbors, the Mauro family, just moved to Texas.' He didn't say what city. I said to him, 'You have to be kidding me. Get me the phone number!'"

Larry called the Mauro family. He knew the son, Joey—they had been best friends in New York—but he didn't know the family. When Larry called, Joey answered the phone. "'Joey, its Larry from New York,' I told him. 'Are you in Dallas?' Joey said, 'No, we're in some town called Richardson, which is a suburb of Dallas.'" Larry flipped.

That night, they ended up all having dinner in Joey's home because his Italian mother insisted that they come. Yes, Italians like to cook. The Norths had been eating hot dogs from the mall and cheap two-dollar buffets, so they were thrilled to have a home-cooked meal.

When Larry's mother walked into the Mauro home, she turned white as a ghost. Larry wondered what was wrong. Staring at a woman sitting on the sofa, his mom said, "What are you doing here?"

The woman looked at Larry's mom and said, "What are you doing here?"

Larry's mother said, "This is a family we know from New York." The woman sitting on the sofa was a friend of the Mauro family but had also been helping my mother all day at Jewish Family Services. This was a completely bizarre coincidence.

The Beginning of an Entrepreneur

The next day, Larry went to work for the Mauro family's swimming pool business. This was the beginning of Larry's quest for success in Texas. He built swimming pools during the hottest summer recorded in Texas history, working weekends and holidays until he was able to save enough money to get his mother get on her feet. Within ninety days, they were able to save enough money to get an apartment. "Seeing that woman in that living room was salvation for us," said Larry, "and, mostly likely, where a higher source wanted us to be."

Reconnecting with Irv

After two years, Larry felt it was appropriate to reach out to his father. He had been released from prison and, ironically, ended up in Vegas from the '70s to the '90s. "Being the kind of guy he was, when he heard my voice, he said in his thick New York accent—excuse my language—'How in the fuck did you do this to me?'" said Larry. "I was about seventeen or eighteen years old. And I said, 'Wait a minute. Time out. Let me tell you something. I'm gonna hang up in ten seconds. You know, I'm happy to communicate with you and talk to you because you are my father, but know this: you are not and never will be the most important person in my life. I am, and my mom and my brothers are.'"

They ended up seeing his father in Vegas in 1991. Irv was not in good shape. He was holding the only legitimate job he'd ever had: driving a cab. He had been stricken with cancer, so Larry and his brother went to go bring him back to Dallas. "I always say it takes courage to forgive. You can't tell people whom they should or shouldn't forgive, but you can take the chance with those that you choose to." They set their father up in a hospice, where he was expected to last about forty-five days. He ended up living for thirteen months. This created some closure between him and the rest of the family.

Larry credits a lot of his passion for fitness to his mother. She was a founding member of Overeaters Anonymous. "I grew up training to be sensitive and kind to people who struggled with eating or weight problems," said Larry. His mother was tormented and ridiculed not just by his father but by her own family when she was a child and young adult. For Larry, he felt that that made for great ambassador training. A lot of people in his industry tend to be a little holier than thou, always focusing on their washboard stomachs. He's always taken a more gentle and nurturing approach in his messaging.

Larry's mother turns eighty-five this year. She is a thirty-year cancer survivor and an amazing woman who keeps busy with various book clubs, major clubs, water aerobics, and yoga. "She is just a ball of love."

So, as you can tell, Texas was not strategic at all for Larry. He had his concerns about coming to Texas with his Brooklyn roots and very thick accent. But things worked out well for him.

Fitness Stardom

Larry ran *The Great American Slim Down* infomercial in the '90s. With more than $150 million in revenue and 1.5 million customers, it was a global sensation. His radio show has run for ten years, and he has three best-selling books: *Get Fit*, *Slimdown for Life*, and *Living Lean*. If you read any of his books or listen to his radio show, you'll see that he doesn't browbeat people. It's all about fitness and overall health maintenance.

Larry's success didn't come easy. His first book got rejected more than two dozen times. A small publisher finally picked it up, and as luck would have it, his book made the local best-seller list, staying in the top ten for almost two years.

For many years, he used to get compared to the "Body by Jake." He and Jake Steinfeld are both Jewish and resemble each other somewhat. Larry used to watch him on the show *Lifestyles of the Rich and Famous* and said to himself, "I can do this in Dallas." That's exactly what he did.

He was twenty-one years old when he started, and if he wasn't the first trainer in Dallas, he's definitely in the conversation. He was certainly the first one to scoop up all the early publicity. Larry was a performer. Every time you turned around, he was in the local newspaper or on the cover of magazines. He had a persona, and he performed it. He had a following long before social media, speaking to thousands of people around the world. "You couldn't take the microphone out of my hand. It's sort of my drug of choice."

Next-Level Networking: Ross Perot and Norman Brinker

Dallas, Larry credits, is fertile ground in which people can create something out of nothing. Just this year, his brother Alan launched KetoMed.com and, after only one show, already has ten thousand orders on autoship. He might end up getting fifty or sixty thousand for this product alone. I don't know too many people who could've pulled off getting this product off the ground anywhere else. Yeah, maybe he could've done it elsewhere, but Dallas is unique.

You have to put a few other pieces together. Larry was a bouncer from the time he was a teenager to his midtwenties. At the time, the places he worked at were by far the most popular in the history of Dallas. He was a connector who was outgoing and willing to do anything to talk to people. He had a strong likability and made a lot of friends in the city. "To this day, you tend to run into the same seven hundred people wherever you go in Dallas," said Larry. It's a big city with more of a small-town feel.

Today, he does high-level private-equity deals, all because of the relationships he's cemented over the last three and a half decades. While he wouldn't necessarily say he couldn't have done what he did somewhere else, he admits that, as a regular, hardworking person, it would have been difficult. Dallas is a little more open to start-ups and entrepreneurs; people are always willing to coach and listen and help. "That is one thing that's great about Dallas," he said.

Larry's mentors include some of the most prominent people in the state. Self-made billionaire Darwin Deason is one and happens to be one of Larry's best friends today. The late Ross Perot Sr. and Norman Brinker were customers at his first health club in 1989. It was located in the most prestigious shopping center in the Southwest, Highland Park Village. You can imagine the connections possible in the highest-income zip code in the five-state region; you are going to get exposed to people who are successful. "Reciprocity is a powerful law. I have always been able to help other people, and it has come back to me."

Larry's family is clearly extremely important to him. In our interview, he couldn't stop talking about them, which said a lot about him. He bragged about his brothers, one of whom retired at thirty-six years old—one year short of his goal. When Larry first landed the lease at Highland Park Village in 1989, his younger brother was blown away that he was able to secure a lease with no money and no credit. When his brother asked him how he'd done it, Larry answered, "Don't worry about it; it's just been my dream, and now I'm going to fulfill it." Larry then passed the question on to his brother, asking him what his dream was. His brother's dream was simple: retire at thirty-five, travel the world, and live the good life. Today, his brother is building a little home in Mexico an hour south of Cancun—in other words, in the middle of paradise.

Becoming a Dallas Icon

Larry was vocal about giving Dallas credit for his success. "I couldn't have done this if it weren't for this city," said Larry. Larry acquired his first gym after getting a request from the owner of Highland Park Village, who wanted Larry to train him. Larry told him he couldn't do it because he lived in North Dallas, far away from Highland Park, where the client lived.

The client was the legendary Henry S. Miller. To solve the problem of location, he helped Larry start his gym in his building. At the time, Larry knew nothing about the business, but it was apparent that Miller knew something was special about Larry. He allowed Larry to sign a lease without doing a background check. "Not that I had bad credit—I just had no credit," Larry added. Larry hustled $30,000 from friends to refurbish the gym.

The gym opened in 1989, and by 1995, Larry's career was in orbit, with international infomercials, a best-selling book, a four-star restaurant, and speaking tours. From the ages of twenty-seven to thirty-seven, he had the Midas touch. But none of it came easily. He faced adversity and tough decisions, but to this day, Larry has no regrets.

Being in Texas was everything to him. "How could somebody in a major market go in unannounced and get a radio show? That's unheard of." In terms of how Larry got his TV and radio shows produced, he gives all the credit to Dallas's business culture: big enough to be a big market, small enough to be able to connect at the local level. He literally walked in off the streets and got his show. And the good news is, it hasn't changed that much. "Dallas has gotten bigger, but it hasn't changed that much. I see people of all ages doing extraordinary things here."

Larry turned fifty-eight just the week before our interview. His focus is now on his radio show and his family. He's interested in continuing to help with the SM Wright Foundation. SM Wright is a black minister with whom Larry has been working for twenty years. When he hosted the first Christmas in the Park at his church in one of the very poorest neighborhoods in Dallas, about three hundred people showed up. Today, this event has morphed into an auto exhibit attended by more than one thousand people. Today, Larry is friends with congressmen, senators, and local politicians, and he feels like he's a part of the community. In the next ten years, he plans on getting much more involved locally to try to make the city better. "It's a great city, but it's not perfect. We can always make it better."

Chapter 17

Running with the Big Dogs

T. Boone Pickens

When I first started Y Texas, I partnered with CBS KRLD on an event in Dallas. I asked their famed radio personality, David Johnson, whether he could arrange for T. Boone Pickens to come to our event and speak about the energy market. Boone accepted the offer.

We filled the room with about fifty executives. David interviewed Boone, as it was apparent he'd done several times before. Boone started by joking that he had to leave in ten minutes to catch the Oklahoma State–Kansas Jayhawks game, which was going on at about that time. The station manager was a Jayhawks fan. In kind fashion, Boone ribbed him about the Jayhawks going down—then admitted he'd never bet against them in basketball.

I worked closely with his public-relations guy, Jay Rosser, on that event. They were a class act, and Boone won over the crowd, as he usually does. I gave him a bottle of wine and thanked him for the timely information on oil and gas prices, which, of course, played out as he'd predicted.

"I firmly believe in the free-enterprise system and the energy the entrepreneurial spirit generates. America has more entrepreneurs than any other nation, and Texas has more than any other state," says Boone, the only Texan (until disproven) who became a billionaire after age seventy.

"I'm a geologist, and geologists are optimists by nature—as are Texans. Sure, you drill some dry holes, but you always know you'll hit on the next one."

Like others who were not born in Texas, he says, "I got here as fast as I could." When he was in high school, his parents moved to Amarillo from Holdenville, Oklahoma. "For me, it was the beginning of a beautiful friendship. I've lived in a number of Texas cities: Amarillo, Corpus Christi, Houston, and Dallas, where I moved in 1989."

He even thought of running for governor in 1990. "Begging out of that notion was the best decision I ever made. It's hard to become a billionaire in public office. Legally, anyway."

Geology and Basketball

Boone attended Texas A&M his freshman year on a basketball scholarship, which was not renewed. Then he transferred to Oklahoma A&M (now Oklahoma State University), where he earned a degree in geology in 1951. Years later, in 2006, after he had given an NCAA record $176 million to OSU, Texas A&M's *12th Man Magazine* named the decision to not renew his $25-a-month basketball scholarship as one of the top ten mistakes in Aggie history.

"I had to smile about that," he says.

After graduating from Oklahoma A&M, he worked for Phillips Petroleum for three years before deciding he needed to strike out on his own in 1954.

Striking Out on His Own

"It was a risky move," he says. "Gone were the corporate credit card and car. I was twenty-six, married, with two children and a third on the way. But I was betting on myself. And I believed in myself. That's another trait that sets you right in Texas. I spent more nights than I care to remember sleeping in the back of my Ford station wagon while on the hunt for oil lease opportunities in the Texas Panhandle. Before too long,

I realized that I wanted more than this one-man band, but I wanted it on my terms."

In true Texan style, he borrowed $2,500 and, with two other investors, formed an oil and gas firm called Petroleum Exploration Inc. in 1956. This company would evolve into Mesa Petroleum, one of the largest independent oil and gas companies in America. By the 1970s, he'd figured out that it was cheaper to expand reserves via Wall Street than to undertake costly and risky worldwide drilling initiatives.

"I love being an underdog, the roar of the crowd, and the cohesion of a fit, well-run team," he says. "I've always tried to innovate in the energy space."

The Largest Corporate Merger in History

"In the 1980s, we challenged Big Oil, and big American business in general, to drastically restructure to meet the times."

Mesa's offer to Gulf Oil was the biggest and most publicized deal of his life at the time. It resulted in the largest corporate merger up to that point in history—valued at $13.2 billion—and more than four hundred thousand Gulf shareholders reaped profits of $6.5 billion. There had never been anything like it in the annals of Wall Street. Upstart Mesa changed the whole dynamic of mergers and became a landmark in the history of acquisitions. Why such activity began in Amarillo, Texas, instead of in New York said volumes about the corporate system that Mesa was shaking up.

Mesa appeared on the scene with new determination, an ability to devise its own financing, and an entrepreneur's view of how to restructure the lumbering, hallowed giants that, to that point, Wall Street had coveted and feared offending. Eventually, all seven of the major oil companies underwent restructuring, benefiting their shareholders.

Fitness Pioneers

Mesa also brought national acclaim to Texas through its fitness campaign, becoming a corporate model in the process.

"I believe that physical fitness creates a better, more economically sound workforce and workplace. In 1979, we built a thirty-thousand-square-foot fitness center worth $2.5 million at Mesa Petroleum in Amarillo and instituted a corporate wellness program, available to all employees and, later, to their spouses. There was no executive locker room. I was right there daily, wearing our standard program participant's blue sweats and gray T-shirt, pounding away on the racquetball court or on a stationary bike."

Mesa was the first company to be accredited by the Cooper Institute for Aerobics Research, founded by internationally renowned fitness pioneer Dr. Kenneth Cooper in Dallas. In the process, Mesa earned the title "Most Physically Fit Company in America" in 1985. Furthermore, the program significantly reduced the company's health-care costs and employee absence rates.

"I've continued that commitment throughout my career," he says. "When I turned eighty, I gave my personal trainer a concise three-sentence job description: 'keep Boone alive.'"

After leaving Mesa at sixty-eight, he and a small cadre of determined entrepreneurs built BP Capital into one of the most successful investment-fund operators.

The Pickens Plan

Boone spent more than thirty-five years traveling to Washington and asking presidents and legislators to formulate a comprehensive energy plan for America while US oil imports climbed from 24 percent to almost 70. In July 2008, he finally decided to take his case for lessening the country's dangerous dependence on OPEC oil to the American public. Thus, the Pickens Plan was born. The project's message was that any viable domestic resource—including wind, solar, and natural gas—should be brought to bear.

"We crossed the country with this crusade," he says. "Again, a campaign that originated in Texas—not Washington or elsewhere—resonated with people and influenced the national dialogue. We are in much better shape today than in 2008."

Pickens's Philanthropy

"Finally," Boone says, "I believe that I was put on this earth to make money and to be generous with it."

Although Boone cherishes his Oklahoma roots and has been active in philanthropic efforts there—as academic buildings, a stadium in Stillwater that bears his name, and a museum that contains the Oklahoma Hall of Fame can attest—in Texas, he has forged dynamic relationships big and small and nurtured incentivized campaigns that have helped changed the face of health and medical research, treatment, and services; of entrepreneurship; of life for kids at risk; of corporate health and fitness; and of conservation and wildlife management.

"I am deeply proud of those commitments," he says.

His most cherished spot on earth is in Texas, of course. Mesa Vista Ranch is a sixty-eight-thousand-acre slice of the Texas Panhandle. "I've welcomed game changers from across the country there for long discussions on how to best maintain the greatest country in the world."

A reporter once asked him whether he considered himself an Oklahoman or a Texan. His response? "Both!"

Like many ardent transplanted Texans, Boone celebrates both its accomplishments and its promise. And he hopes that he has made the best of both worlds.

Advice from Boone

Texas is a business-friendly state, but if you want to run with the big dogs and make a mark here, you need to know yourself and have a plan ready. And if you're going to run with the big dogs, you've got to get out from underneath the porch.

Chapter 18

Texas Pride with a Return on Investment

Mike Rawlings, Former Mayor of Dallas

When Dallas mayor Mike Rawlings met with companies interested in Texas, his direct approach didn't pull any punches. He had two closing points. The first: "If you don't want to give your shareholders the best return on investment, you might not want to come here." He backed this up with the fact that DFW-based companies have outperformed the S&P 500 by up to 30 percent. I found this remarkable.

Then, the closer: "Don't come here if you don't want to give back to our city." Now, I'm sure he was more subtle in making these points, but it worked, and it's true. Facts don't lie. He often told businesses that business in Dallas is a participation sport: if they don't get involved, they won't have fun and will be outcasts. If you haven't already heard that theme in this book, you're hearing it now. In fact, most companies do participate. Companies here have a chance to make a difference, giving them a great return on their time—and, as Mayor Rawlings stated, on shareholder dollars!

Mike Rawlings was the mayor of Dallas from 2011 to 2019, the longest tenure of any Dallas mayor in nearly sixty years. He was actually born in Texas in a city called Borger, but he did not stay long. When he was a young boy, his parents moved the family to the Midwest and then to the East Coast, where he attended Boston University. His formative years were spent in New England, which I believe is where his accent comes from. He also happens to be a Red Sox fan, which is not one of his more endearing qualities.

Mike returned to Dallas in the '70s, a time when jobs were plentiful in Texas but few and far between up east. He had nothing to his name but a beat-up Volkswagen. His career blossomed, taking him from a position as advertising executive at a local Dallas advertising agency, TracyLocke, to the role of CEO of Pizza Hut. After Pizza Hut, he and a few partners went on to form their own investment firm, CIC Partners. In 2011, he was elected mayor of Dallas.

This year, Mike ended his two terms as mayor. I didn't plan on interviewing any politicians for this book, but I knew his journey in Dallas would be valuable to you, firstly because of his two terms as mayor and also because of his long experience of working his way up the corporate ranks. As a radical centrist, as he puts it, in a city that votes Democratic with a deep Republican executive voting base, he was the right guy for the job. His experience and approach to collaboration are in line with the culture in Dallas, and he is someone you should know about should you decide to move here.

Mike is a larger-than-life figure, tall in stature with a confident voice. He is part of a long line of Dallas mayors who have been instrumental in building the city into the economic powerhouse it is today. Those of us who live in Texas will be familiar with Dallas freeways such as the RL Thornton and the Woodall Rodgers, both named after past mayors. Thornton was a banker and businessman whose claim to fame was, among other things, the expansion of Dallas Love Field Airport. Rodgers's tenure included the construction of the Central Expressway, a north-south thoroughfare connecting downtown Dallas to the northern suburbs, all the way up to McKinney.

Will a future Dallas structure bear Mayor Rawlings's name? Only time will tell. However, there are already many accomplishments he can take with him. He managed Dallas during its safest time in decades, saw us through a soaring economy, and was steadfast in his pursuit to improve parks and green spaces in our city of cement, including Carpenter Park, Harwood Park, Pacific Plaza, the West End, Fair Park, and Klyde Warren Park, which sits over the Woodall Rodgers Freeway. His investment-banking acumen helped guide the city through a tough issue with the Dallas Police and Fire Pension fund and was influential in bringing private investors to the table to fund major projects in Dallas that helped bridge eastern and western Oak Cliff.

In my opinion, Mike Rawlings's legacy will be in his ability to bring people and ideas together. He's a good communicator, with a marketing background that helped him position ideas to the public. His executive experience helped him prioritize and accomplish objectives while keeping a keen eye on the financial responsibilities of running a city. Still, Mike found clear differences between being mayor and being a CEO. "Being a CEO is like being an inch wide and a mile deep. Being the mayor is like being a mile wide and an inch deep." With the breadth of responsibility that comes with being the mayor of a city as large as Dallas, you just can't go deep on everything.

I've talked a lot in this book about how our corporate leaders are some of the most collaborative you will ever see anywhere. The same is true of Mike. Two of his qualities in particular shine through to me and will leave a lasting legacy on the region. The first is his passion to grow the southern part of Dallas. GrowSouth, as he named it, is a generations-long initiative to bring investment and economic opportunities to the south of the city. The program is comprehensive, but the key to its success is bringing residents, teachers, and companies together to bring up the community. From helping bring parents into Dallas Independent School District parent-teacher organizations to luring businesses into opening shops in the area, it is a ground-up, entrepreneurial approach to governing that is still in its early stages.

The second, which might seem more trivial, is his working relationship with Fort Worth mayor Betsy Price. If you are not from Texas, this will be interesting to you. For as long as I've been in Texas, Dallas and Fort Worth have always had sort of a sibling rivalry. This rivalry dates back decades; some tie it to the naming of the Dallas–Fort Worth Airport. If you have a Dallas area code, good luck doing business in Fort Worth. The feeling was mutual in Dallas. There has always been a sense of animosity toward each other.

In recent years, Mayor Rawlings (a Democrat) and Mayor Price (a Republican) began building a working relationship. They traveled the world to market the DFW area to companies looking to relocate to the region. Instead of having their two cities compete against each other, they courted companies to move wherever they wanted, as long as it was Dallas–Fort Worth. It took strong personalities to break the cycle of rivalry, and the region is benefiting from it.

Texas Pride

In my interview with Mike, he showed a clear passion for keeping Texas pride alive. If you've ever listened to him speak, you know that's no secret. And while he has been involved in some of the largest corporate relocation transactions in the state, he feels the contagious nature of that Texas pride is what really lures people here. "Folks that didn't get a dose of that are a little jealous and drink the Kool-Aid as fast as they can."

His own family came here from Alabama and Tennessee in the 1840s, looking, as he put it, "to grab a piece of that brass ring." He didn't grow up here pledging to the Texas flag in school, but he claims to be more Texan than most believe. He relishes Texas's Friday night lights and admits to jamming to Waylon, Willie, and the boys.

When he talks to businesses looking to move here, he is very candid in explaining to them that we clearly beat any other state in the pride department. "I tell them that you have to work hard, and you have to be a nice person." I think that says it all, and I agree with him 100 percent.

Mike is very involved in meeting with companies all over the world that are looking at the DFW area. He works closely with the Dallas Regional Chamber and delegations of executives to sell the region. He was at the forefront of many conversations with Amazon, talking with them frequently in collaboration with the chamber. He gets very personal with company executives, demanding they bring a spirit of collaboration and an expectation of rolling up their sleeves to help grow the region responsibly.

Mike admitted that Dallas knocks the ball out of the park when it comes to traditional relocations, touting its cost of living, its ability to do business, and how gifted it is in its location. He lays claim to the entrepreneurial spirit of our forefathers, who built a city with no port, harbor, or mountains. The crux of their vision was to develop the DFW International Airport, which could fit the entire city of Manhattan within its perimeter. Today, the DFW region is home to three Fortune 10 companies, twenty-four Fortune 500 companies, and forty-three Fortune 1000 companies, including ExxonMobil in Irving, AT&T in Dallas, and American Airlines in Fort Worth.

The Future of Dallas

Since I moved to Dallas in 1993, the city has transformed a lot. Skyscrapers are everywhere, and the highways I grew up on now have overpasses and, unfortunately, some tolls. I am biased, but I believe the Dallas area, even more so than Houston, has the greatest opportunity for global impact in the world. It has a diverse set of industries driving its economy, with sprawling cities reaching all the way up to the Oklahoma border. But with this responsibility will come challenges as it tries to redefine itself and grow up. The city of Dallas is getting more urban and less rural.

This state loves challenges, and it approaches most things through a free-enterprise, capitalistic culture. The mayor is on the front lines of that. As Mike departs from office, he's passionate about paying attention to the southern part of Dallas and getting those who are well educated to participate in lifting up those who are not. As he said, it's a participation sport. That is what he means.

This isn't done by giving money to everyone. "That's not how we do things in Texas," said Mike. But it's done by bringing out the self-starter in each of us. His view on education is that we must be intellectually honest with ourselves in realizing that our next big challenge will be to increase the level of educated and skilled technology workers. So if you're reading this part and have the skills, know that there's plenty of work for you in Dallas.

Advice from Mike

Mike wants to challenge corporate leaders to attack the talent shortage like they would any other challenge—and to do it in a Texan fashion. The reason we don't have Amazon is that we didn't have a deep enough bench of tech talent. He encourages our faith-based communities to get involved and invites them to be part of the Texas miracle. "Xenophobia is not biblical," said Mike. He closed by urging us to ask ourselves, How do we stay pure to our independence while being inclusive and aspirational as well?

Dallas provided Mike a platform through which to accomplish big things on a big scale. New England is more quaint—not the platform you need to scale ideas. "The key to being rich is to be a genius, then scale it," said Mike. There are many examples of such people here, including Mark Cuban, who started with a small start-up in Dallas, Stanley Marcus, who reinvented the retail business, and the late Herb Kelleher, who changed the way Texans traveled. "It's not who you know but what you can do and what you can accomplish," said Rawlings. "The opportunities are here for you."

Chapter 19

Oh, Thank Heaven for 7-Eleven

JOE DEPINTO, CEO OF 7-ELEVEN

Texas is home to some of the most iconic brands in the world, and 7-Eleven happens to be one of them. The company was founded in Texas ninety-two years ago. As a fourteen-year veteran of the company, their current fearless leader missed out on the first seventy-eight years; however, if you are relocating a billion-dollar company to Texas or moving here to lead one, Joe can provide some sound advice for you.

7-Eleven, like most global companies, sells more overseas than in the United States. But being domiciled in Texas has many benefits, including, of course, no state income tax. Just as importantly, it has a corporate community that needs your expertise and involvement on many levels. This applies even to those companies that have been here for ninety-two years. As someone who moved here himself, Joe can provide some tips to help you in your transition. If you are on the fence about whether to come, he might even fly out to convince you. He has been instrumental in making that happen with many companies during his time here in Texas. He's what you'd call an ambassador.

The History of 7-Eleven in Texas

On June 29, 1927, the Southland Ice Company filed as a for-profit corporation with the Texas secretary of state. Its location was Oak Cliff, Texas. As the company's name indicated, they sold ice. That was it. When an ice dockworker noticed that everyday consumers were running out of staples like bread, eggs, and milk, he started to offer those on the side. The company owner, Joe C. Thompson, took note and began adding these incidentals to his product offering. Soon thereafter, the business grew to twenty-one retail ice docks, and the concept of the convenience store was born.

Almost twenty years later, the business's name was changed to 7-Eleven—a reference to the operating hours, 7:00 a.m. to 11:00 p.m. every day of the week. Twenty years after that, in 1966, the Slurpee took the world by storm. The inventor of the frozen margarita machine, a Dallas restaurant owner named Mariano Martinez, cited the Slurpee machine as his inspiration for changing the face of the classic cocktail.

Today, 7-Eleven still calls Texas home after ninety-two years. With more than sixty-eight thousand stores worldwide, this trademarked brand is still one of the most recognizable in the world. Unfortunately, they still don't sell margaritas.

Joe DePinto—From the Prairie State to the Lone Star State

Joe DePinto has been the CEO of 7-Eleven for the last fourteen years and couldn't think of being anywhere else other than Dallas, Texas. He's a native of Chicago who now roots for nearly all Dallas sports teams— with one exception. You might still find him singing the classic Steve Goodman tune "Go Cubs Go" during the baseball season.

Joe came to Dallas in 1986 after graduating from West Point and being stationed at Fort Hood, which is located in Killeen, Texas, halfway between Waco and Austin. "It was a cultural change for me," said Joe, "but I immediately fell in love with Texas."

Joe grew up in Chicago, then spent his college years in New York. He didn't know any culture other than a fast, urban one. "As a youngster, I thought of Texas as a dust bowl, hot and a little slow," said Joe. When he got here, however, his impressions changed immediately. Since then, Joe has spent all but nine years in Texas, when his career temporarily took him back to Chicago and Louisville. Eventually, he made his way back to Texas, like everyone does.

Family

Joe attributes his smooth transition into Texas to his wife's family. Their Southern hospitality and the welcome they gave him really helped. His wife is a Corsicana, Texas, native. Two of their kids are native Texans as well, while the other two were born elsewhere during his nine-year hiatus away from Texas. The two kids who were not born in Texas still can't get over the fact that they are not natives. Joe attributes this to how the public schools teach Texas history. "They get a lot of pride from that," said Joe. I agree with Joe. Every Friday, Serene Hills, my kids' elementary school in Austin, brings all of the students into the auditorium to sing Texas's state anthem. The students know it word for word. It always gives me chills when I hear them sing it. I wonder if other states do that. I doubt it.

Joe's sister moved to Texas when her husband took a job in Houston. She had been a Chicago resident her whole life. When her husband's job later took him out of Texas, they decided to rent out their Houston home—a sign that they might someday return. Another good sign is that their kids decided to stay. Continuing the DePinto invasion of Texas, his parents have moved to Texas, and his brother is also poking around with the idea of coming to Texas. The point here is to consider your extended family when you make the move here. Getting them to follow might be easier than you think.

Recruiting Talent to 7-Eleven

As the leader of one of the most recognized companies in Dallas–Fort Worth, Joe touts the business-friendly nature of Texas as one of its best attributes. He couldn't say enough about the Dallas Regional Chamber and the Dallas Citizens Council, both of which advance business causes through economic development and public policy advocacy. He also gave much credit to Mayor Rawlings for his leadership within the business community. If you move here, expect to have a personal relationship with your mayor and other politicians. As Mayor Rawlings put it, it is a team sport.

Also plan to get actively involved with boards and other community activities. It will be expected of you, and quite honestly, you will enjoy it. Joe is involved with a number of high-powered organizations and boards, providing the expertise we need to help drive our economy. For example, Joe sits on the ownership advisory board for the Dallas Stars. Dallas Stars CEO Jim Lites asked Joe to help promote the team throughout the business community. I would image Joe had no problem with this, having been a former hockey player at West Point who grew up in the tundra of Chicago. When Joe had to leave Dallas in 1992 because of a job relocation, he was very disappointed because, with the Stars coming to Dallas, he had been gearing up for some great pro hockey. Now, he's helping promote the team.

Joe is also involved with the Southwestern Medical Foundation, the George W. Bush Presidential Center's Military Service Initiative, and the SMU Cox School of Business. He is also the chairman of the board for Brinker International, a public company that owns, operates, and franchises more than sixteen hundred restaurants in thirty-one countries under the names of Chili's Grill & Bar and Maggiano's Little Italy. Give back, and it will pay dividends.

Recruiting Talent

When it comes to recruiting talent to 7-Eleven, the local universities bring a pool of candidates who are skilled and interested in staying local. "Right now, I am knee deep in finding IT and digital talent," said Joe. He can find talent locally, but when it comes to applicants coming from out of the state, the cost of living and the Texas lifestyle is easy to sell to them. "For our executives and franchisees, the DFW airport is in close proximity to their Irving headquarters and store support centers," said Joe. That makes travel and access to the area easy, which have a big impact on quality of life. Throw in Friday night lights and the public school system, and you have a recipe for success.

7-Eleven relocates hundreds of people into Texas, so I asked Joe whether he gets any objections. He had to think about it for a minute. Then it came to him. "The heat. Yes, the weather is what I hear about most." I asked how he counters that problem. His answer, "I ask, 'Would you rather have the heat or the cold?'" But honestly, he feels people object only because the heat initially catches them off guard. After a short while, they get accustomed to it.

Then I asked what about Texas, in his experience, most surprised the people he's talked to. That answer came a little more easily. "The growth of the region and the cost of living." Compared to the rest of the US, the cost of living is incredibly attractive. All of this means a lot to people, according to Joe. A lot of people have relocated to Texas with 7-Eleven, and many of them will never leave—as long as we have air conditioning.

The Texas Economy

During Joe's tenure as CEO, 7-Eleven has experienced a major growth spurt, both domestically and internationally. They are in the process of entering their eighteenth country, India, later this year. They also continue to perform feasibility studies in South America, Russia, and Eastern Europe. Expansion will continue at 7-Eleven, and Joe feels good about it.

The 7-Eleven brand is also growing locally. "We are thankful to be here," said Joe. He reminisced about a few of the Dallas locations they have operated in over time. They used to be headquartered downtown at Cityplace; then they were an anchor at One Arts Plaza. He was amazed at how large the Arts District has grown over the last ten years. Today, the company resides in Irving, Texas, home of seven Fortune 500 companies. Irving–Las Colinas has more Fortune 500 headquarters per capita than any other city in the US.

Joe saw Texas grit shine through during the major economic downturn from 2008 to 2010. Even then, he would peer out his window and count ten to fifteen cranes visible across the cityscape, as if all were business as usual. "Think about that—growth occurring during a major economic downturn." He has seen Dallas explode with condos and apartment buildings. He wished he had a camera to capture it. I'm sure we could track one down.

As a small-box retailer, Joe often reminds his prospects of the growth projected for the state. The fastest-growing region in the United States is the Texas Triangle, which extends from I-35 in Dallas to San Antonio, from I-10 to Houston, and from I-45 back to Dallas. The Rio Grande Valley is up there as well, around number five on the list. Today, 7-Eleven has roughly twelve to thirteen hundred stores in Texas. Franchising is strong in the state, so they also benefit from that. The iconic brand is recognized in most cities, especially in Southern California, Florida, and the Northeast. I was happy to hear that, with the recent acquisition of Wilson Farms in the Buffalo and Rochester area,

7-Eleven is growing again in Upstate New York. When I was a kid, my uncle Savario Boffoli, affectionately known as Uncle Sonny, franchised a 7-Eleven near Englishtown, New Jersey. We all looked up to him as the entrepreneur of the family. Joe said that brand recognition—that attitude of, "Oh yeah, 7-Eleven is back"—should help for sure.

Texas Pride

A strong sense of pride and work ethic are part of the culture in Texas. It's a place where people are looking for opportunity and for a lift up to a level from which they can achieve new heights on their own. "Texas is not a handout state; it's a lift-me-up state" is what the fourteen-year veteran CEO of 7-Eleven told me when I asked what advice he would give to newcomers.

Joe made an interesting point that I agree with: he feels the Texas culture comes from two things. The first is the indoctrinated pride Texans learn at a very young age. It stays with them through life. The second are those who immigrated to Texas from Mexico and now call Texas their home. They came here hungry, looking to make their lives better, and Texas provides the opportunities they seek.

Joe remembers that when he started working for 7-Eleven, he realized how well the culture and values of Texas lined up with what he saw at the company. People all over the state and within the company worked with pride and with an interest in making things better.

Over the years, the company has had many opportunities thrown at it by other states—or even other countries—trying to incentivize them to move the headquarters out of Texas. They always turned such offers down. Given the cultural and financial benefits of being here, they couldn't think of being anywhere else. Oh, Thank Heaven for 7-Eleven.

Advice from Joe DePinto

Do your homework on neighborhoods and school systems. The neighborhoods here are great and family friendly. Pick one with schools at the K–12 level if you don't plan on moving too often. My kids have done well in the public school system here.

Get involved. Be active in the community, and give back. It will come back to you many times over. Growth is a powerful thing. When we prosper, it allows us to do other things. Businesses giving back makes for a vibrant area.

You will be shocked at the amount of home you will get for the price. The quality of the buildings for the money they cost is something I hear about all the time.

I've known a lot of folks who have grown up here. They will have no problem talking to you. I have also met a lot of folks who have moved here. You will have a bond with them because you both come from someplace else.

There's a saying in Texas to use if you move here: "I wasn't born here, but I got here as fast as I could!"

Chapter 20

The Story behind the Story

Tracye McDaniel, President of TIP Strategies

Without the six principles laid out in this book, no marketing or incentive plan would have gotten Texas to the point it is at today. That said, Tracye McDaniel has witnessed many of the efforts the state has made over the last twenty years to shape the story behind the story of relocations into Texas.

From 2000 to 2001, the state shifted its messaging to keep up with other states that were aggressively recruiting companies, including offering financial incentives for them to do so. This was the tipping point after which companies started to see the potential of moving to the Lone Star State. Once we executed on a strategy to educate companies about the benefits of doing business in Texas, it opened the floodgates. Today, we are reaping the rewards and challenges of this strategy's success.

Who Is Tracye McDaniel?

Tracye is a major player in Texas economic-development circles. She happens to be a fourth-generation Texan, too, which kind of makes her qualified to talk a little about Texas. She originally wanted to be a journalist, but a short career working for an NBC affiliate was enough for her. After graduating from UT, she volunteered at a chamber, and the rest was history. In Tracye's words, "My career chose me, and I loved it every step of the way."

Since then, Tracye has led either tourism or economic-development efforts for five governors: one in New Jersey, Chris Christie, and four in Texas—Ann Richards, George W. Bush, Rick Perry, and our current governor, Greg Abbott. She began her career as the CEO of Capital City Chamber of Commerce (Austin's black chamber of commerce), which led her to support the creation of the Texas Association of Black Chambers of Commerce, growing twenty-eight different chambers comprised of either women or African Americans. She then went on to be COO of the Greater Houston Partnership (GHP), one of the largest business associations in the country. It began as a hybrid of a chamber, a world trade association, and an economic-development corporation, which merged to form the partnership. Tracye helped raise the first $32 million dollars used to create the platform.

Her career took her, for a brief stint outside of Texas, to New Jersey, where she helped lead an initiative called Choose New Jersey (a partner in the Partnership for Action) for Governor Chris Christie. Tracye returned to Texas in 2015 at the request of Governor Greg Abbott to lead economic-development efforts for his administration. In 2018, Tracye returned to the private sector as president of TIP Strategies. The same year, she was also elected chair of the International Economic Development Council (IEDC), the world's largest membership organization serving the economic-development profession. It boasts more than five thousand members across the United States, Canada, Europe, Australia, New Zealand, and elsewhere. Tracye sits on the YTexas advisory board and has become, to me, a mentor, confidant, and friend.

The Tipping Point

Many pundits speak about the migration to Texas that occurred in the early 1800s, when Texas was still part of Mexico. It is said that during the Panic of 1819, many US residents fled to Texas to escape debt. On their doors and fences, these people wrote the letters GTT, which stood for "gone to Texas." Today, many still use the GTT acronym in a joking manner when picking up to move to the Lone Star State.

When it comes to corporate relocations, however, it was not far in the distant past that few companies were posting GTT on their business doors. Don't get me wrong; it was always seen as a place of opportunity and independent thought, but the phones weren't ringing off the hook with businesses looking to move here. When Tracye first started with Ann Richards, she remembers that the state's tourism marketing strategy was focused on bringing in visitors to generate business. They leaned on the popularity of JR Ewing and the TV show *Dallas*, hosting elaborate parties with shirts bearing the Texas flag, cowboy hats, boots, buckles, and cheerleaders. Tracye said, "It was all about that look. We had to own it, and it was real. No other state carried such a folklore and pride."

Tracye realized that while this strategy was gaining attention for attracting tourists, our state was flat at recruiting companies. We had to build a value proposition for job creation. Governor Perry shifted the approach, hired economic-development professionals, and gained support from the Texas Legislature to design a department within the governor's office to build a lead-generation strategy focused on jobs. "We were looking to build a more sophisticated and aggressive economic-development strategy," said Tracye, "based around not only attracting businesses but building an ecosystem in which they can grow." This swing didn't happen overnight, but collaborations and partnerships with other government agencies and the private sector helped create one of the most competitive programs in the country.

The Perry Administration

Each governor Tracye worked with had a different perspective on economic development, but she believes this development was really born under the Perry administration. The state needed a promoter and a peer-to-peer—meaning governor-to-CEO—relationship with those job creators. Rick Perry was the right guy at the right time.

My experiences with Governor Perry echo Tracye's. My foray into the economic-development industry began under his leadership as well. I saw him in action with CEOs in New York, Chicago, and California. "Move to Texas, we'll take good care of you," he would tell them. He would make personal phone calls whenever he needed to. I remember a time our delegation went to New York City with a full agenda. The next day, the news contained trash talk by the mayor of NYC about how Governor Perry and a delegation of Texans had marched into the city to lure businesses out of the state. That evening, Governor Perry made a very impressionable comment to a crowd of New York business owners. These were not his exact words, but in essence, he said, "Listen: if you don't think other states are knocking on our business owners' doors and asking them to come to their states, you'd be a fool. Every governor and mayor should be asking CEOs what they need—and selling them on what they can offer. They are the job creators. I am just doing my job, just like any CEO would." That really stuck with me.

According to Tracye, the turning point with Governor Perry involved discussions with Toyota about building a manufacturing plant in San Antonio. Leading up to this event, they had been surprised to learn that even though Texas had everything companies were looking for, employers were still choosing other states instead. "When asked why, employers would say we weren't competitive with other states," she said. Texas was still passive in its approach to giving employers what they were seeking: incentives.

At the time, Texas, as a state, had no incentives to offer. Forget about incentives—when executives wanted to come in and look for a site, the state couldn't even afford to show them around. Any money spent would be public funds, so they didn't want to be frivolous. But when the Toyota expansion came across their desk, they had to find a way.

Toyota in San Antonio

Texas had had several tourism offices throughout the world, including one in Japan, but by the mid-1990s, most had been shut down, except for the offices in Mexico and Japan. The director of the state's Japan office from January 2001 to June 2013 was Ms. Naoko Shirane. She was a huge advocate for Texas. Shirane was instrumental in developing and fostering the business relationship between San Antonio and Japan for more than twenty-eight years.

When Texas began negotiations with Toyota, she became very involved and, according to Tracye, was a big part of Toyota's decision to come to Texas. So, with her help, some good Southern hospitality, and the scraping up of some incentives, San Antonio won the bid for the Toyota plant. A descendant of a well-known Japanese family, she possessed the diplomatic skills to accomplish the unthinkable. According to Tracye, she had the tenacity to build and nurture long-term relationships and to strengthen the international partnerships.

The administration learned a lot through this project, including that it takes hard work, attention to detail, and incentives to at least get businesses to the table. But the most glaring lesson was that there needed to be a personal connection with decision makers. That relationship really helped sell the heart of Texas—and if there's one thing we do well, it's that.

In this case, Texas didn't have the best incentives. But without them, we wouldn't even have been at the table. With an already probusiness climate and a sense of pride bigger than anywhere on the planet, Texas could not be touched. This began the era of Texas incentive funds, such as the Texas Enterprise Fund and Emerging Technology Fund, sending an aggressive message that Texas was wide open for businesses.

Project Emmitt

In 2004, Texas Instruments was looking to move their headquarters. And before you assume they would stay in Texas, remember the adage about assuming: don't do it.

I would find it odd for Texas Instruments to be headquartered in any other state, but business is business. The company was looking to move some assets out of the state. At the same time, Emmitt Smith was considering leaving the Dallas Cowboys. In corporate relocations, it is commonplace for projects to take on code names to protect confidentiality, so Tracye thought it would be fitting to call this one Project Emmitt.

"I wanted to name it Project Emmitt because we were bringing it home," she said.

Then the strategy began. Some say the deal with TI was one of the biggest economic-development agreements at the time in the United States. The state and local community worked collaboratively to keep TI's $3 billion investment in its chip fabrication plant in Texas. The University of Texas at Dallas played a major role, as it wanted to attain tier-one status in research. "This was truly a public-private relationship," said Tracye. The state, the university, the chamber, and other local organizations worked together to make it work. Eighteen months later, the state brought together a team to announce the investment from Texas Instruments.

A Probusiness Mind-Set

In 2013, New Jersey governor Chris Christie publicly announced that he was hiring Tracye McDaniel to lead the economic-development strategy of his state. The program was called Choose New Jersey, and its focus was on sending a message that New Jersey was open for business. Choose New Jersey was a part of a three-prong approach to economic development that formed the Partnership for Action.

New Jersey was a bottom-ranking state in terms of business climate. It had high corporate taxes and was a labor-union state, something Tracye had never had to deal with before. New Jersey was making an effort to show the business community its willingness to work with them through Choose New Jersey, an initiative led and funded by the private sector. Tracye's biggest challenge was the mind-set of the local business community. She had thought this would be the easiest part. Not so.

She didn't expect this going in, but it turned out that her biggest task was to change the dialogue around the way business leaders thought about their position as contributors to the economy. In Texas, CEOs were engaged in policy making, philanthropy, and leadership. It was expected. In New Jersey, it was quite the contrary. There was a strong philanthropic mind-set, but businesses were highly regulated by the government. Tracye needed to flip the mind-set to show that employers were the ones contributing to the tax base and creating jobs and that elected officials were not entitled to run their businesses. This was a long process, but she immediately saw a change once that way of thinking caught on.

In Texas, we might take it for granted that businesses have a voice, but that's not the case in every state. So if you're moving here from out of state, know this: leadership is expected of you, and you have a voice through dynamic organizations like YTexas, the Texas Association of Business (TAB), and chambers of commerce, along with business-friendly elected officials.

Takeaways

What I hope you take away from this, the story behind the story of company relocations to our state, is that when we say Texas is business friendly, that friendliness goes far beyond low taxes and regulations. It is friendly because we know where our bread is buttered, and our goal is to make it easy for you to hire fellow Texans and have a voice in our process.

Whether you believe incentives work or not in this day and age, it is undeniable that they play a role. Regarding the dollar amount of incentives needed, each situation is different. Without them, though, despite our other offerings, we would lose out. With them, we win. And we win a lot.

So you might ask, then, "How does this affect me?" Well, when Toyota entered San Antonio, it started by creating three thousand jobs. According to Tracye, by the time the deal was in its second or third year, another three thousand jobs had been created as a result of the company's supply chain. Small businesses were created in, sustained by, and relocated to the area as a result of Toyota's investment.

"What we learned is that proximity is key for product and service delivery," said Tracye. To take it a step further, San Antonio worked hard to help Toyota employees integrate. The city built schools for both Japanese- and English-speaking students and embraced the contribution Toyota was making to their community. Today, Toyota is still a major contributor to the local workforce, working with the Alamo Colleges District system and the University of Texas at San Antonio to build a pipeline of students in the region skilled and educated at all levels.

Today, the Texas Instruments headquarters still remains in Richardson, Texas, and the University of Texas at Dallas has a flourishing technology program that creates fertile ground for future technology professions. Having begun as a research arm of Texas Instruments, in 1961 the founders bequeathed the center to the state of Texas, officially creating the University of Texas at Dallas. Fewer than forty-seven years after the school's founding, the Carnegie Foundation classified the university as a doctoral research university with "highest research activity," the school having achieved that ranking faster than any other school in Texas.

Advice from Tracye

In Tracye's experience, businesses judge their locations based on a responsible public sector that provides a certain level of continuity and certainty for their business. They want a state that is as fiscally responsible as they are. If they see mismanagement or fraud, they will shy away.

Pay attention to the larger employers in your area of interest for supply chain opportunities. Companies like Exxon, AT&T, Toyota, and Dell are constantly expanding in our state, creating more opportunities for smaller firms.

With more than three million workers, Texas has an outstandingly skilled workforce. Our biggest challenge is to continue to build a talent pipeline so that companies can obtain the best talent and stay competitive.

If you are moving products around the world, mobility is a huge advantage of Texas. Our airports and rail systems are some of the best in the country. Our transportation network is sound and is always innovating to keep up with demand. Governor Abbott's bold leadership ensures a Texas where economic prosperity is obtainable, encourages greater job growth, reins in skyrocketing property taxes, elevates our education system, and reforms government to allow the full potential of the Lone Star State.

Our cost of living is affordable, so attracting talent will be easier than in other places. Our schools are better than you might think. And our culture is inclusive. People can find their tribe here. Look into these things to determine whether Texas will be right for your employees and their families.

PART THREE

Takeaways

Chapter 21

Your Cheat Sheet

There are many lessons to be learned from the stories in this book, but to make it easy for those speed readers who like to get to the point, I'll break them all down for you in this chapter. For a more comprehensive list of resources for doing business in Texas, visit YTexas.com.

Start with Why

So, what's your why—the true reason you want to move? That should be the number-one thing you ask yourself when looking to relocate. Almost every story in this book had a different why—a different *real* why, that is. Dig deep, then look to the future. The two should align.

Ed Trevis, the CEO of Corvalent, saw an urgent need to get out of Silicon Valley because of his inability to attract talent. Corvalent, at least at the time, was more of a hardware company in the industry, and he couldn't afford to give his people six-figure salaries. But his real why, unbeknownst to his entire staff, was that he didn't think the company would make it if they didn't move. He saw the future, and he took action.

Andy Roddick had two whys. Firstly, he just wanted to go home and retire in Austin. He put an offer down on a house on Lake Austin two days after winning the 2003 US Open. His second why was business rather than personal: he wanted to realign with a new set of donors who could take his foundation to the next level. He needed a demographic who could accommodate the growing needs of his foundation. He also wanted to home in on a local need and put all his efforts into changing an entire city in need. In five short years, he has grown his impact from eighty students to more than fifteen hundred a day.

Larry North's why was to escape a less-than-stellar family life. Texas just happened to fall on the map by circumstance. When he arrived, he had only a short-term plan, and that was survival: support his mother and younger brothers, then figure out the rest later. He hustled, found a few handy friends like Ross Perot, and is now a world-renowned fitness guru.

So—start with why. And no, "cheaper" and "warmer" are not the result of digging deep. Answering that question will be the beginning of a successful journey.

Location, Location, Location

According to *The Yale Book of Quotations*, the infamous phrase "location, location, location" originated in a 1926 classified ad in the *Chicago Tribune*. We all know it as a cardinal rule of real-estate investing. However, I'm not necessarily referring to real estate when I use it here. Choosing a location for your business should take into account many factors—real estate, of course, being one of them.

As should be clear from this book, many people—myself included—believe that people are at the heart of corporate relocations. Many others, however, seem to forget that. As a business owner, when choosing a state, city, or country for your relocation, you need to understand this principle. If you are an employee, I hope your employer understands it. Toyota, for example, centered their entire twenty-eight-hundred-person corporate relocation around this premise. Their move was a corporate restructuring of several of their affiliate companies, bringing them all into one central hub. They had to consider how each of these affiliates would work together, collaborate, and innovate. They not only examined where their supply chain was but also notified other suppliers of their move. Many of these suppliers then came with them in order to keep the account. Lastly, and most importantly, they considered their employees, including where they would live and how long of a commute they would have. The CEO knew that people's productivity at work was paramount and that they had to give them work-life balance in order to make the relocation a success. There was a lot on the line because they were moving thousands of people into Texas from Kentucky, New York, and California. They even took into account feedback from employees on how to build their headquarters to accommodate a big fear of, of all things, tornados.

In the end, they chose Plano as the location of their new million-square-foot corporate headquarters. Of course, with one million square feet, real estate played a role, but it definitely was not at the center of the decision. The location had to meet other criteria too.

Jim Garvin, the former CEO of biotech company CytoBioscience, chose to relocate his headquarters to San Antonio. In his words, it was a no-brainer. After looking at several cities, they stumbled upon San Antonio through a reference from a client. They were surprised to find that more than thirty-five hundred biotech companies were located within a fifty-mile radius of the city. That, combined with some of the most affordable housing in Texas, made his decision a piece of cake. Had he not known those numbers, he would never have chosen San Antonio over Florida or Canada, both of which offered the company millions of dollars more.

Lessons learned: Look farther than real estate in determining your location. Make a list of your priorities and criteria for success. Determine a general location, and then begin your real-estate search.

You Don't Win on Emotion; You Win on Execution

Tony Dungy, one of my favorite Pittsburgh Steelers players, once said, "No excuses. No explanation. You don't win on emotion. You win on execution." When it comes to corporate relocations, this couldn't be any more true. One thing I can promise you is that there will be plenty of emotion.

If you learn anything from the individuals who contributed to this book, notice that they all had a plan—and executed it. You might not have a plan in place yet, and that is fine. But you do need to execute—and quickly. Yes, if you're coming from a coastal city, you might find that many things are slower in Texas than you're used to, but business is not.

I hear way too often from newcomers that they had to get settled in first and didn't sit down and work out the details until a few months later. They didn't have time to meet and network or learn about what was happening around them. I've known way too many clients who ended up looking for work within six months after a botched move. Keep in mind, the board will always want you to do twice as much in half the time. If you are responsible for a move, do your best to build in a contingency plan and communicate that to the board. The costs pile up, and time flies, and it will be your ass if things don't meet expectations. There is nothing worse than catching your board off guard.

Notifying Employees, Stakeholders, and the Public

One of the most difficult things you will likely have to do is notify all of your stakeholders. The timing of who and when is critical, and it's different in every situation. You will have to balance a lot of factors.

First, when negotiating incentives with a city or state, there will often be a "quiet period" during which you will be sworn to secrecy.

Large corporate relocations often involve these. Amazon is the most relatable story; for more than eighteen months, their exploratory committee needed to remain silent and neutral during the decision-making process. I have no idea when they actually knew where they were going, but they did a pretty good job of playing poker. For smaller companies, like Ottobock, this can be more difficult. As Andreas Schultz told us earlier, someone in the company leaked information that ended up negatively affecting the outcome of Ottobock's city incentives, and it cost the company lots of money.

Next, identifying who in your company will be involved in the decision-making process. In Toyota's case, only eleven of the twenty-eight hundred people to move were part of the underwriting, so to speak. They did a great job of keeping things under wraps. Even the mayor of Plano said to me, in a separate interview, "All we knew was it was Bob from California."

Then you need to notify the team. When and how to do this is something only you will know. At Toyota, employees were notified up to three years in advance. Your company might not have that luxury, so balancing out that notice is important. Many in our study seemed to give about three months' notice.

At Ottobock, this was very challenging for Andreas, even though the owner of the company flew in from Germany to give "the talk." Not knowing what to expect, he planned for "the talk" by hiring armed bodyguards. When the employees were all offered the option to move, he knew that as soon as he blurted the words, "We are moving to Austin," everything else would be a blur. In Andreas's case, he planned for the unexpected. Fortunately, there was no gunfire. A carefully planned strategy in this area will not only help with the move but will keep the team together once you land.

Last, and certainly not least, is notifying the public. You need to carefully plan this process as well—and don't put the cart before the horse. I heard it rumored that the son of one of the executives of a large company let the cat out of the bag on Twitter by saying something like, "My dad is moving to Texas with his company. I gotta move." This was on the eve of the big announcement. On another occasion, a press release about the move went out before the incentives were approved—which ended up killing the deal. I think the person in charge of that lost their job. Handle this part with care. It could cost you dearly.

Negotiating Incentives and Understanding Their Implications

We will not delve too far into incentives in this book. They are a factor; however, I will tell you that some of the interviewees who did receive incentives told me that they weren't the only factor in the final decision. Several interviewees actually chose Texas despite competing locations offering more. One company even told me that, in hindsight, they would have never taken them in the first place. Again, every situation is different.

Still, incentives do and should play a role. Again, I didn't delve into this in my interviews, but I do know that if Texas (or any state, for that matter) didn't have some incentive offers on the table, they most likely would not be in the running.

Financial incentives can be offered by the city and state of Texas. Incentives come in many different forms, including tax exemptions, reimbursements, grants, loans, and tax credits. Be careful, as incentives can be clawed back if you do not meet certain hurdles. Keep this in mind, because if these hurdles do not align with your vision, you will spend more time meeting the requirements of the incentive than executing on your plan. There are also many programs available for training and recruiting talent, so please research them all. For state incentives, go to BusinessInTexas.com for up-to-date programs. For city incentives, most larger cities have an economic development group that can help you. Hire a professional who knows this business. It will be a lifesaver.

Do the Research

Be meticulous in your research. Your employees, family members, and investors will appreciate it.

Know the Neighborhoods and Real-Estate Costs

The prices in Texas are low compared to most metropolitan areas throughout the US.

However, there are some parts that can go toe to toe with the best of them. Austin and Dallas proper, for example, have some of the highest-priced zip codes in the country. San Antonio and parts of Houston are very affordable. Most suburbs will have prices that are attractive but getting up there. In my experience, most families will likely head to the burbs.

Property taxes play a major role, adding up to 3 percent of the appraised value of your home. So if you're getting a $300,000 house, property taxes could go as high as $9,000 per year. Research this for your people.

Know the Commercial Market

Consider all the options. Believe it or not, shared workspaces are becoming more common in corporate relocations of all sizes. WeWork, for example, is exploding in their enterprise market, taking down some buildings and leasing out thousands of square feet to companies as large as Google. This could be an option if you are looking for a full-service location.

Leasing, both for the short and the long term, is very common in Texas. The tenant-rep industry was essentially founded here by Dallas Cowboys quarterback Roger Staubach. In Texas, having a tenant rep is essential to finding an ideal space and to negotiating lease terms and tenant improvements. The title business in Texas is somewhat regulated and different than in other states. For example, you will need a title agency (not just a lawyer) to close on real property. And yes, there is a cost for that, and it's not negotiable. The fees are regulated. The real-estate market is booming in Texas, from the Panhandle to the valley. Seek out options.

Purchasing, building, and developing are longer-term and higher-risk endeavors. Not all cities are equal in how they manage building codes. Some are more onerous than others. In whole, Texas's regulatory environment, even in building, is very favorable. Land development gets a bit more tricky.

Texas has been known to land some hefty relocations, resulting in large takedowns of land for headquarters, distribution centers, and manufacturing facilities. If you are willing to wander out of the major metros, you'll find that areas like Fort Worth, San Marcos, southern San Antonio, and the Woodlands are very attractive options. Housing is extremely affordable in and around these cities (probably with the exception of the Woodlands), and incentives are there for the taking.

Large developers like Hillwood (a Ross Perot company), KDC, and Endeavor are creating major centers from corporate headquarters and distribution centers in industries including aviation, cybersecurity, and biotechnology. San Marcos is home to a biotechnology complex affiliated with Texas State University; Fort Worth has AllianceTexas, an inland port for distribution and aviation; and San Antonio has Port San Antonio, formerly the Kelly Air Force Base, which is being repurposed for cybersecurity, robotics, and engineering firms all looking to put down stakes in Texas.

Keep an eye out for juicy incentive deals that have a little more risk than you think. I know of one manufacturing company that took down an entire business park to build a new headquarters. The city gave them attractive incentives to develop more land than the company needed. In hindsight, the CEO realized that he took on more risk than he'd anticipated and had to spend more time and money building out the park than running his business. In the end, it's going to work out. But if he were to do it over again, my bet is that he wouldn't.

Anyway. A good broker can help you with the nuances of Texas real estate. There is much to go around and plenty of incentives out there to allow you to scale your businesses for decades to come.

Compare and Contrast

When shopping for a new location, don't be afraid to compare and contrast potential states' and cities' incentives, prices, and market conditions. I will say that, all in all, Texas usually comes out on top. Also know this: if Texas knows you are interested in them, they will come out with guns blazing (not literally). Ed Trevis with Corvalent couldn't believe that, with a company as small as his, then governor Rick Perry made a visit out to his plant in California. He couldn't even get the mayor of his own city to pay a visit. Texas sent the governor!

Organizations like the Texas Economic Development Corporation, now known as Go Big in Texas, are very aggressive in courting businesses and will often bring convoys of business executives and state dignitaries such as the governor, the secretary of state, or state senators.

I cut my teeth at the TEDC, making many house calls in cities like Chicago, New York, California, and even Beijing, China. We would fill town halls at local restaurants. In New York, I recall us getting some heat from the mayor about us coming to invade his city. Governor Perry got up at dinner and said, in essence, "Hey, you don't think people are coming into our backyard asking our companies to look at their cities?" Economic development is a competitive sport—and if you don't pay attention, your businesses will leave.

I find this rather timely, seeing as Amazon has announced that they are pulling out of the New York HQ2. Whether those elected officials were speaking on behalf of their city (or just on their own behalf), it clearly made Amazon realize that this was going to be a place where they would not be welcome. I can promise you that that would have not been the case in Texas.

I remember the first TEDC executive director who embraced me with open arms: Tracye McDaniel, after she first took over the position on appointment by Governor Abbott. The first time I spoke with her was by phone in a parking lot. I'd pulled over for our scheduled call. She had just spent a few years helping then governor Chris Christie with a program she'd launched called Choose New Jersey. I'm not sure how many companies are choosing New Jersey, but I know a lot are choosing Texas—and I gather that that is why she came back.

Identify Your Criteria

Once again, there is no better example than Toyota. When I spoke to their CEO, Jim Lentz, he offered to send me the list of criteria he'd used in choosing Texas. Each was weighted differently. Review the list of Toyota's criteria in chapter 2, and think about whether any apply to you. If so, learn from the best.

Know the Local Talent Pool

The best investment of time you can make is to speak to local recruiters. Then, visit the community college systems and major universities. They all work together. Don't forget what I told you: ask and you shall receive. Your industry will tell you where the talent is coming from, how much you need to pay them, and what they will demand. If you're in Austin, you'd better buck up for talent. Even with an unemployment rate of less than 4 percent, believe it or not, you can find them, though it will cost you. Consider perks such as flexible hours, stocks, warrants, and other nonfinancial benefits. They will go a long way.

If you are a skilled tradesman, you will never go a day without work. Plumbers, electricians, mechanics, nurses, and truck drivers are in high demand. In my opinion, this demographic should be flocking to Texas. You will get good pay, always have work, and be within earshot of an affordable house. Oh, but don't call your union boss; he doesn't exist here.

The Dallas County Promise is a coalition of school districts, colleges, universities, employers, and communities that have joined forces to help more Dallas County students complete college and begin careers. The program has plans to scale across the state. Just another example of out-of-the-box thinking from our state leaders.

Size Up Local and State Governments

In addition to local incentives, you need to examine your local and state governments to see where they stand on issues related to your industry. Think back to what happened to Amazon in New York. They should have seen that coming a mile away.

Budget for Twice the Cost in Twice the Time

Maybe, for Donald Trump, a move will come in underbudget and on time—but for a corporate relocation, I wouldn't put my money on it. Even for the Donald.

Most of the unforeseen costs that companies incur during corporate relocations are based in the human capital, the countless trips back and forth, and the sales lost during the transaction. If you are receiving incentives, you might be able to absorb some of these. If not, they could eat you alive. In addition, if you are building or developing property from afar, good luck. Lastly, if your people either are not coming or are heading for the door during the process, you could be in a world of hurt. Plan for the best, and budget for the worst.

Network, Network, Network

I can't stress this enough. Your network will be everything in Texas. I built my entire career off of nice people who helped me, even with my New York accent. If that isn't convincing enough, then reread the chapter about Larry North. Larry built his entire empire off of a network including a few familiar names like Ross Perot and Norman Brinker.

I could write a whole chapter on networking, but to boil it down, start with your local chambers of commerce and economic development corporations. I don't know how many times I've heard newcomers say how impressed they are with our chambers. They are the real deal. Yes, they have events with small talk and power networking for hairdressers and real-estate agents, but their programs are extremely comprehensive. And, actually, you will need a hairdresser.

In fact, the chambers and economic development corporations in all regions of Texas—including the Greater Houston Partnership, the Austin Chamber, the Dallas Regional Chamber, the Fort Worth

Chamber, and the San Antonio Economic Development Foundation—are powerhouses. Know their CEOs; they will help you with open arms. State-run organizations like the Texas Association of Business, the Governor's Commission for Women, and the Texas Economic Development Corporation are all must-joins as well.

Pick a Cause and Run with It

If you're going to make a mark in Texas, philanthropy should be in your plan. Everyone has a cause that is meaningful to them. Everyone helps each other out. It many ways, philanthropy will define you. If you do not have any passions or have left most of them behind, organizations like the Communities Foundation of Texas are great places to learn about all the nonprofits there are in Texas. In every interview I conducted for this book, everyone was blown away by how philanthropic Texans are. Aligning with a cause will also empower your people to realize they are serving a higher purpose. That is what millennials and members of Gen Z find most appealing in an employer.

Embrace Limited Government

Texas is a limited-government, probusiness state, often requiring employers to help solve problems that governments traditionally would. Employers here prefer that. They enjoy a government that gets out of the way and allows them to do their job, which is to create jobs. Unions, other than in the public sector, are virtually nonexistent.

Our legislature meets only once every two years, and we are one of only four states with a biennial budget and legislative session. In writing a budget for the biennium, the legislature has to make sure it balances, meaning they appropriate only as much general revenue or rainy day funds as the comptroller estimates will be available. Balancing the budget is widely considered to be the foundation of state fiscal practices. As more and more people move into the Lone Star State, this is something we will be challenged with. The system requires us to be responsible and to spend only the money we have, with a rainy-day fund that actually serves the purpose of saving for a rainy day. Rainy days in Texas are when crude oil prices are low, which affects revenues in the state. After the sharp decline in state revenue caused by low oil and gas prices in the 1980s, Texans amended the state constitution to create a fund designed to save revenue collected in good times to pay for services when revenues declined in bad times.

If you come from a high-government state, this will be something you should be aware of. Where to spend this money continues to be a point of contention on both sides of the aisle. If you get involved in local politics, understand that overspending is not in the cards at the state level, so innovative thinking and a working partnership with employers can be a best practice.

Talk to Your Neighbors

Believe it or not, talking to your neighbors will pay big dividends. If you don't get to them first, they will get to you. Don't be afraid to talk to strangers, even in an elevator.

Bring a Good Culture, and Keep It Intact

Nearly every company profiled in this book came in with a solid culture. Hilti exemplified a company-wide culture, here and abroad, that put the employee first. When they moved their headquarters from Oklahoma to Dallas, that culture was already in place. If you need to build a new culture or abandon a bad one, you will certainly face challenges. Having a good culture in place will make life a lot easier. Check your culture at the door—and fix it quickly, preferably before you arrive. If that is impossible, you can easily build a good culture here if you understand the society described in this book. Hire smart, embrace our probusiness environment, and you will be off to the races.

Consider the Families Impacted

Think about the trailing spouses, partners, children, and parents when considering your move. One of the eleven members of Toyota's transition team was the CEO's wife. She was able to look at the process through the eyes of a trailing spouse or partner and foresee issues they would likely face. Children, whether in school or in search of a college or a job, should be paid attention to.

Make accommodations for the people you are moving to visit the new location and kick the tires. They will not only feel important but could also uncover things that you might not have thought of.

Don't Forget your Hometown

Even if you are picking up and moving your entire headquarters out of state, don't forget where you came from. If it's in the cards, leave an office there. Keep some longtime employees who can't make the move with you. Stay in touch with local politicians and influencers, as you will likely have clients who feel abandoned. Even a local address with a few employees and a phone number can be enough to keep them at bay. Don't forget your roots.

Get Involved in Sports

Whether you like it or not, sports are huge in Texas. Consider investing in some luxury box seats or even a suite. If the cost is too much, look for a partner. The American Airlines Center in Dallas hosts some of the hottest acts in the nation. Austin now has Formula One racing and just landed an MLS team. Football is popular, from Pop Warner on up to the Cowboys and Texans. Scouts will look at your son or daughter at a ridiculously young age. It's just how we roll. College sports are just as big, if not bigger. Understanding "gig 'em" and "hook 'em" is recommended. When the Mavs, Stars, Rockets, Spurs, Rangers, Astros, Cowboys, or Texans are in the playoffs, their cities rock. Business booms, and the beer flows. Embrace it. So far, I have been able to kick the Knicks for the Mavs and the Rangers for the Stars, but the Rangers and Cowboys haven't been able to steal my heart from the Yankees and Steelers.

MLS soccer is also gaining steam in Texas with the support of the Hunt family, who essentially brought professional soccer to Texas.

Women and Children First

Make women and children a priority. Carefully look at the area's school options, whether public, private, or charter. Also look at the preschool market. If all the parents in a family have to work, the costs can get up there. Some neighborhoods are more likely to send their kids to private school, which will add a few bucks to your cost of living. So if prices are really good in a particular neighborhood, chances are that the schools might be subpar.

The higher education system in Texas is one of the best in the nation. State schools are the best bargain, but getting in will be a challenge. Schools such as the University of Texas are incredibly selective, typically accepting students who perform near the very top of their graduating class. But from Houston up to Dallas, the state has many options. If a four-year university isn't in your or your child's plans, our community college system is aligning with employers to provide certificates and skills training to get students working quickly. There are also many nonprofits in Texas focused on teaching coding and technical skills at a very affordable cost. All in all, make this a priority in your search. We do.

Texas is the number-one state for female entrepreneurs and is making a go for the top spot for women-owned businesses, so much so that Texas has the Governor's Commission for Women, which is specifically centered around empowering women to excel in the workforce. More than eleven million businesses in the US are owned by women. In Texas, they account for about 20 percent of the state total and more than 5 percent of annual payrolls, according to the US Census Bureau's 2014 survey data.

Many women have leadership roles in our state, so if you had any doubts about that, I hope you feel better. In anything, there is always room for improvement, but overall, there is plenty of opportunity here for women. If you are an accomplished woman business owner, executive, or employee, prepare for good things. If you are aspiring, you've come to the right place.

Know the Competition; It's Friendlier Than You Think

In most US markets, your competition is the enemy. Maybe it is in Texas, too . . . but in many cases, its friendly competition. I recommended you know your competition—personally. I've made many introductions between competitors over the years, and many of them have found ways of doing business together. Several years ago, I introduced a CEO who had moved to Texas to lead a major interior design company to one of his competitors. They happened to be sitting next to each other at an event. Within a few months, they'd become friends, and but for a couple of dissenting board votes, they would likely have merged. My point is that you never know what might become of knowing your competition. Either way, friend or foe, you should at least know what they are up to.

Build a Pipeline of Talent through Community Colleges

The community college system throughout the state is relevant. Many of the colleges in the system offer free training and market research to local employers. Get involved with your local community college, and attend some of their events. It is a great feeder system into many of the middle-skilled jobs needed here in Texas. They offer certifications and degree programs that can help fill jobs immediately. The community college systems in all regions are actively involved in speaking with employers about what their current and future needs are in terms of skills. They play a major role in our educational system.

Know the Hidden Costs

Understanding all of the costs your business will face in Texas is an exercise worth going through. Texas remains one of the lowest-cost states in which to do business, but in some industries, it can get pricey in certain areas.

While we do not have a corporate income tax, we do have what we call a franchise tax or margin tax. Franchise taxes do not kick in until you have at least $1,000,000 in annual revenue. They also do not apply to most partnerships and sole proprietorships. This tax is based off of your revenues, not your profits, so if you are in a low-margin business, this could be troublesome. Recent legislative sessions have looked into lowering or even eliminating this tax. So far, no luck.

At a rate of 6.25 percent, sales taxes in Texas are a little above average. Local cities can also add up to 2 percent to this tax, putting your overall state sales tax at more than 8 percent. Of late, there has been discussion—not yet determined—regarding the Wayfair tax, so add that in as a potential cost if the state enacts this new tax. The Wayfair tax is one states are now looking into regarding online sales of products going through the state. If I were a betting man, I would say we will pass on that. But I've lost a lot of bets in my life.

Property taxes in Texas are some of the highest in the nation, approaching 3 percent of the appraised value of your home or building. Texas does offer a homestead exemption on your primary residence, giving you a significant discount on property taxes. They also offer discounts to veterans and seniors. In order to get the homestead exemption, you have to live in your home on January 1 of that year. So if you move in after January 1, you can claim the exemption the following year.

Property taxes are local taxes, not state taxes. Some cities have higher rates than others, so look into this closely as you peruse neighborhoods. This could be a significant number.

The gasoline tax in Texas is $0.20 per gallon. The state has not raised this tax for several years, making it one of the lowest in the nation. Once you get here, you will notice the difference when you fill up your tank.

On the personal side, we have no state income tax. Because of our robust economy and the deep bench of businesses in Texas, we have revenues to make up for the lack of personal and corporate state income tax. So when you hear the words "drill, baby, drill," know that this is one of the reasons our cost of living is low.

Energy prices in Texas are also some of the lowest in the nation. Texas has a deregulated electricity market that allows competition among the state's electricity providers. We also operate on our own electric grid outside of the rest of the US. This open market is what keeps these costs down, allowing technology companies, data centers, and large manufacturers to flourish here in Texas. You'll also see the savings in your personal electric bill.

Embrace Innovation

Texas is known as an innovative state. From our early beginnings, there has always been something in the air that pushes us all to find better, more efficient ways of doing things. The energy, health-care, and technology industries are the best examples of this. Texas leads the nation in renewable energy sources, particularly in wind energy production, is also a leader in cancer research and biotechnology breakthroughs, and is home to many of the technological advances making our lives easier. The Texas 5G Alliance is advocating for the 5G connectivity of the future in Texas. They are educating Texans on the exciting possibilities of 5G technology and the infrastructure that will be required to meet the demands of smart cities. The goal: to make us all more competitive in the global marketplace. So don't be surprised if one of your competitors is trying to do something to break the mold in your industry. If you can't beat 'em, join 'em

Know College Football

Sorry—this is Big 12 country. The esteemed collegiate athletic conference is headquartered right in our backyard in Irving, Texas. Know who is winning and when Texas–OU weekend is. It will help you make friends and not feel like an outcast on the golf course. If you know where Texas A&M, UT, Baylor, Texas Tech, and TCU are in the standings, you should be fine.

Know Where to Get the Money—and Not

Many say that unless you are looking for an oil-and-gas or real-estate investment, you will have a hard time finding funding in Texas. To some extent, that is true. We have been getting better, but still have work to do. Private equity is available in Dallas and Houston, but in other markets, it's rather more scarce. In 2018, Peter Thiel, infamous for his investment in Facebook, announced he was relocating the San Francisco venture capital firm he cofounded with Ajay Royan to Austin. The firm, Mithril Capital Management LLC, is an online news site. This could be the sign of more venture capital coming to Texas.

Royan was quoted in TechCrunch as saying that they picked Austin because of its lower costs and diversity of thought as compared to the East and West Coasts. As for his experience so far in Austin, Royan said, "I was impressed by the friendliness and gastronomic offerings." He also said that while in Austin, most of the people he'd met were registered Democrats and half of them owned really nice guns. These qualities are not considered contradictory at all. San Francisco–based venture capitalists packing heat sounds scary, but only in Texas, I guess. So keep in mind that you don't need to live in Silicon Valley to raise money there. Employ people here, and get the money there—if you have to.

Where we have room for improvement is in the area of early-stage venture funding. However, we are making a run for it. The Austin Technology Council is a leading collaborator. All of the major markets in Texas are investing heavily in the start-up community through organizations such as the Dallas Entrepreneur Center (DEC), Capital Factory, Station Houston, and Geekdom in San Antonio. The start-up world in Texas is hot. But you might have to go to Silicon Valley and New York for the dough, at least for now. If you want to go wildcatting for crude or build the next skyscraper, you have plenty of runway.

The commercial-banking market in Texas is one of our strong points. Every major bank in the world is here, along with a robust group of regional banks to choose from. Relationship banking is not just a phrase here; it is real. So, as a newcomer, buckle up. You will need to prove your worth and integrity quickly. The good news is that there are plenty to shop from. A referral from a friend or a client of the bank will go a very long way here. So, make some friends.

Depending on your industry, grants can be something to look for. Texas has many grant programs. One is called the Cancer Prevention and Research Institute of Texas (CPRIT). It awards money for investment in cancer research. Other programs can be found via our resource guide at YTexas.com/resources.

The angel networks and accelerators throughout Texas are growing a burgeoning start-up environment that is attracting many millennials and members of Gen Z. So, there are funding mechanisms here; you just need to find them and position yourself around them.

Expand in Other Texas Markets

This one is high on my list of recommendations. What most people don't know is that Texas is home to more than one hundred Fortune 1000 companies within our metropolitan regions. Many people who land here will open up an office in, say, Dallas, then later realize that four other major markets are within a stone's throw from their headquarters. To stay competitive, having an office in Dallas, Fort Worth, Austin, San Antonio, or Houston is recommended. At least get four phone numbers, each with one of the following area codes: 214, 817, 210, 512, or 713.

Know the Industry Hot Pockets

If you study areas of industry concentration, you might have a better understanding of where you will fit in best. In the DFW area, downtown is turning into a tech town, with lots of young people taking scooters to work and riding the DART rail. North of Dallas, in Plano and Frisco, we are seeing a plethora of office parks and corporate headquarters relocations. In Fort Worth, with AllianceTexas, we are seeing distribution centers and manufacturing facilities abound. Cities like Irving, being in close proximity to the DFW Airport and affordable housing, are also attracting a wide array of headquarters. Central Texas will continue to be a mecca for technology, while companies are flocking to the northern parts of Austin—cities like Cedar Park, Leander, Georgetown, Pflugerville, and Round Rock—where there is a vast amount of buildable land and lower-cost housing. San Antonio, with its military bases and large veteran pool, is leading the way in biotechnology and robotics. With some of the lowest costs of living and close proximity to Mexico, it still is the place to be for manufacturing and distribution centers. San Antonio is also making a run at it.

As you approach San Marcos, you'll find that a large biotechnology hub has emerged, with Texas State University being the feeder to this sector. Houston is all things energy but is also home to one of the largest medical districts in the US, including MD Anderson Cancer Center. The Port of Houston and access to the Gulf of Mexico naturally make it an oil-and-gas mecca. It is also emerging as a force in start-up businesses, attracting a lot of talent from other large cities like New York, Chicago, and Los Angeles.

Every region in Texas is booming with retail and consumer-based businesses—for our growing population of consumers, of course. Industries such as retail, professional services, and consumer packaged goods are all growing at a rapid pace. If you are competing in this space, get ready for some competition. Texans are loyal buyers, so get your brand out there quickly.

The qualities of these regions go a lot deeper than this, so research your SIC code. You will be surprised at how much opportunity there is almost anywhere in Texas.

Expect the Unexpected

Unfortunately, things happen, and you need to plan for them. I've seen, in more cases than one, an entire company relocate to Texas only for the company to be sold, merged, or acquired shortly thereafter. This also leads to unexpected layoffs.

Whether you are a CEO or an admin, you need to plan for this. After you've uprooted your family, you might find yourself in a precarious position. Do you move back or stay? My recommendation is to stick it out. I have several clients who fell into this situation and stayed. Those who were prepared fared far better. This is another reason to build your network.

Plan for the Weather

This is another top-of-the-list item, judging by the feedback I've received from newcomers. The weather here affects both personal and business life. The summers get really hot. I think it's a dry heat, but others don't. Austin and Houston are a little warmer than Dallas, and Houston is the most humid of them all. It is very common for summers to feature temperatures of more than one hundred degrees for thirty days in a row. What makes it worse is that it doesn't cool down at night. A ninety-eight-degree evening is common during the summer. Winters are mild but do get cold. It will hardly snow in Texas, but Dallas can get snow every couple of years.

In terms of business, plan for a slow summer (unless you are in the construction industry). Olivier Chavy, the former CEO of interior design company Wilson & Associates, stated that he did not expect the summers to be so slow for business. Luckily for Wilson, they had plenty of international business to make up for it. Keep this in mind for your industry. The summers are so hot that a lot of people vacation for most of the season.

Disrupt or Be Disrupted

This is a common threat for nearly all business models. Any and all industries are constantly looking at old business models and determining how to make them more friendly to and centered around consumers. With the influx of entrepreneurs moving from across the globe, you are more likely to be challenged by disruption here in Texas. Examine your business, and ask yourself whether you are at risk of being disrupted. Join the conversation, get on boards, and join your local trade associations to learn about the future of your industry. Tech Titans is a great forum that represents the interests of a quarter million employees through its three hundred member companies in North Texas. Also check out Dallas Innovates, a collaboration of the Dallas Regional Chamber and D Magazine Partners. The Innovation Center in the Cockrell School of Engineering, led by professor of innovation and ethernet inventor Bob Metcalfe, aims to accelerate the impact of faculty inventions by using start-ups as vehicles of innovation. These are just a few that can keep you ahead of the next disrupter.

Hire Local Board Members

One of the first things Andy Roddick did when he moved his foundation to Texas was add local board members. He recruited some of the best minds from companies like Dell to help build the organization. When Richard Tagle was recruited out of DC to run the foundation, he said that what gained his interest was not only Andy's commitment to the cause but the quality of that board. Consider adding a few locals to your board. They will add some local brainpower that will help you not only grow but compete.

Knock the Preconceived Ideas

If I have accomplished anything in this book, I hope you now understand that Texas is not what you might have thought. In fact, my editor (who happens to live in Fresno, California), said, "I can't believe how much I learned about Texas that I didn't know. I've been telling all of my friends about the different regions and industries." Get the preconceptions out of your head (and, more important, out of your employees' heads). Do what Ed Trevis and Jim Lentz did: educate your employees before asking them to move.

Check Out Your Texas Roots—You Might Have Some

On more than one occasion during the writing of this book, I found that many of those I spoke to have some Texas roots, whether through a distant relative or a spouse. Jim Garvin of CytoBioscience, for example, told us that his great-grandfather fought at the Alamo. So ask around, and you might find out you have some Texan in your blood. You might get some street cred too.

If You Have to Leave, Plan on Moving Back

This is a bold statement, so don't take it the wrong way—but if you move, I promise you, you will find your way back. If I had a nickel for every person who tried to leave Texas yet found their way back somehow, I would be a rich man. Seriously, don't burn bridges, because you will come back. So save yourself the hassle, and make the best of your time here. It is where you will ultimately end up.

Consider Extended Family along the Way

When I asked Harry LaRosiliere, mayor of Plano, Texas, what he's regretted about moving here, he said he wished he had tried to get his parents to move here as well. Now, I don't think he thought they would, but you never know. Since I moved here, my mother and sister Janine have also moved. My mother is a registered nurse and moved here with out a job, taking time to settle in first. In no time, she had three offers at major Dallas hospitals. My sister Janine fulfilled a lifetime passion to start a dog-rescuing business. My sister Jennifer and niece Raevyn came for a brief time, and others have poked around the idea. So don't be afraid to ask. They might actually join you.

Know All of Your Health-Care Options

Like our education system, our health-care system is (in my opinion) underrated. Yes, it is not perfect. Look into your options. We have some amazing hospital systems, like Baylor Scott & White, MD Anderson, and Children's Health, that offer affordable and quality health-care services. We have public hospitals, like Parkland, and a slew of clinics and practices that can provide good, affordable health care. But as with anything, you have to research.

Texas Press

For a state as big as we are, there are handful of news outlets (in print, at least) that you should leverage: the *Dallas, Austin, San Antonio,* and *Houston Business Journals*; the *Dallas Morning News*; the *Houston Chronicle*; the *Fort Worth Star-Telegram*; the *Austin American-Statesman*; and the *San Antonio Express-News*. My favorite is *Community Impact Newspaper*, based out of Pflugerville, which has local papers in the Austin, Dallas, Fort Worth, and Houston metro markets. There are many more, but these will get you started.

Events

Texas is becoming a hub for world-class events, and it's growing every year. Houston and Dallas host most major tours; Austin and San Antonio, not so much. Austin hosts South by Southwest in March, bringing more than 289,000 people a year to Austin. That's like a Super Bowl every year. Austin City Limits is in October, and Circuit of the Americas hosts a Formula One race every November. WGC-Dell Technologies Match Play, a major PGA event, is held every March in Austin. This used to be a well-kept secret, but not anymore. San Antonio hosts the Valero Texas Open. Dallas and Houston are always in the running for the Super Bowl or the All-Star game for some sport. DFW hosts the Byron Nelson and the Charles Schwab Challenge, formerly known as the Colonial Invitational, in May, while Houston has the Houston Open—and also hosts the largest oil-and-gas conference in the world, the Offshore Technology Conference, in May.

Chapter 22

Some Fun-Loving Texas "Ediquette"

To close, I figured I would touch on some more casual topics that might help you get through the day as a Texan. I hope you find these helpful.

- Talk to strangers, even on elevators. If you don't, they will start the conversation.
- Under no circumstances should you honk your horn. Ever. You will be alone.
- Pedestrians take right-of-way to a new level. They walk really slow and smile.
- Bars close at 2:00 a.m., so no need to pace yourself.
- Yes, open carry is exactly what it says.
- You are now in CST, so all your favorite shows will be on earlier or later.
- Work hours are 9:00 a.m. to 5:00 p.m., except for in Austin, where you work from 10:00 a.m. to 3:00 p.m., have a workout, then return to work from 6:00 to 9:00 p.m.
- Dress code: If you wear a tie in Austin, you'll lose lots of friends. If you don't wear a tie in Dallas, you'll lose all credibility.
- Dallas to Houston on I-45 is not so bad. For Dallas to Austin on I-35, pack a lunch and bring a cup.
- For interstate business travel, on Vonlane, work all day, and on Southwest, work half of the day.
- In Austin, don't set an appointment before 9:00 a.m. Most people are sleeping or working out.

- There is a barbecue war between Austin and San Antonio. Tread lightly with both.
- If you get a divorce in Texas, as Eddie Murphy once said: half.
- In your first thirty days in the state, you are required to get a Texas driver's license. They are serious.
- Dallas and Houston airports fly direct to everywhere. Austin and San Antonio fly direct to nowhere.
- Dallas, Fort Worth, and Houston highways look like roller-coaster rides. In Austin, we are not allowed to build highways. San Antonio doesn't have enough traffic to require them.
- Mineral rights are liquid gold if you are lucky enough to be sitting on oil.
- No, you cannot buy liquor on a Sunday before noon. If you need to, you probably have a problem anyway.
- In terms of road etiquette, combine NYC and LA, then throw in a little Texas.
- There is no gambling here, but Louisiana and Oklahoma will welcome you with open arms.
- If you want to do business in Fort Worth or San Antonio, you'd better get an 817 or 210 area code, respectively. Other cities don't care.
- To those moving here from the East Coast: yes, you will need a car in Texas.
- From the West Coast: it's still hot, but a dry heat.
- From the Midwest: still just as friendly, and plenty of Packers and Bears bars.
- From internationally: you might have to have your family dry ship you some native food.

About the Author

Born and raised in New York, Ed Curtis relocated to Dallas, Texas, at the age of twenty-five and has happily lived in the Lone Star State ever since. Over more than twenty years as a Texas commercial banking executive, Ed witnessed an increasing number of investors and clientele relocating their businesses to Texas. As a result, he exited the banking industry to form YTexas, an elite business network that helps support, promote, and connect companies that are relocating and expanding into the Lone Star State.

The unified group of YTexas executives has become a go-to resource for the most current insider information about Texas's community, commerce, and culture.

Ed's ultimate vision is to build YTexas to national prominence and to replicate the program in states around the US. Ed lives in Austin with his wife, Staci, and two children.